goal sisters

goal sisters

Live the Life You Want
with a Little Help from Your Friends

Ann Leach & Michelle Beaulieu Pillen

New World Library
Novato, California

New World Library
14 Pamaron Way
Novato, California 94949

Cover design by Mary Ann Casler
Text design and typography by Tona Pearce Myers
Interior cover illustration by Michelle Beaulieu Pillen

Library of Congress Cataloging-in-Publication Data
Leach, Ann,
   Goal sisters : live the life you want with a little help from your friends
/ Ann Leach and Michelle Beaulieu Pillen.
      p.   cm.
   Includes bibliographical references and index.
   ISBN 1-57731-432-8 (paper back : alk. paper)
   1. Women—Psychology 2. Self-help groups. 3. Motivation (Psychology) 4. Self-esteem in women. I. Pillen, Michelle Beaulieu, 1961– II. Title.
   HQ1206.L385 2004
   158.1'082—dc22   2004000559

First printing, April 2004
ISBN 1-57731-432-8
Printed in Canada on partially recycled acid-free paper
Distributed to the trade by Publishers Group West

10   9   8   7   6   5   4   3   2   1

To women everywhere who desire to bravely step out of the familiar and take the leap toward having greater fulfillment in their lives.

Contents

Introduction

You wake up one morning to a loud knocking on your front door. You stumble out of bed with no makeup on and morning breath to boot. As you approach your front door, you hear women whispering excitedly outside. Who are they? What do they want? You unlock the door, open it cautiously, and...

"Surprise!!" Two women holding a bouquet of flowers, a picnic basket, and multicolored bags are standing outside your door.

Not quite awake, you refocus your eyes, yawn, and ask, "Are you the Publishers Clearinghouse ladies? Did I win something?"

"Ah, no, we're not those ladies," beams the blond-haired woman as she offers you the flowers. "We're Ann and Michelle. Didn't your friend from work tell you about us?"

"Friend from work?"

"You know," says the dark-haired woman, "the one who's leaving to start her own business. We're the ones who showed her how to make that happen. We're her Goal Sisters!"

"Her what?"

"Her Goal Sisters. We're here to offer you the same opportunity we offered her: our friendship and a way to make *big* changes in your life."

"Oh, you're *those* ladies! My friend's always talking about you two. You helped her set goals, cheered her on, and checked on her progress."

"Yep, that's us. May we come in and tell you more about how we do that? We promise not to bite."

You hesitate a little.

"We have coffee and bagels. Juice and fruit."

Because you're curious — and you don't have anything to eat for breakfast — you invite Ann and Michelle in. You lead them to your couch, picking up magazines and dishes from the night before, straightening the piles on the coffee table.

"Don't worry. We'll just move things over."

The two women make themselves comfortable on your couch, put down their bags, open their picnic basket, and pass around plates, napkins, and mugs. They've come prepared! After you dump last night's dishes in the kitchen sink, you grab a vase from the cupboard and stuff the flowers into it while making your way back to the living room.

"Gosh, it's great to be here and meet you," says Ann, offering you a cup of coffee. "Your friend told us you're a perfect candidate for being a Goal Sister."

You take a quick sip. "She did?"

"Uh-huh. But before we tell you more, can we get you to do one thing?"

"What's that?"

"We'd like you to keep an open mind," Michelle responds as she passes you the bowl of fruit salad. "Just be open to the possibilities. Will you do that for us?"

"I'll try."

"Great! Okay, Ann, take it away," says Michelle, waving her bagel in Ann's direction.

Ann smiles and bats her eyelashes at Michelle, then leans forward and says, "Okay, here's the scoop: Your friend told us you're pretty happy with your life. You like where you live, you're healthy, you make enough money to pay the bills, and you have a little fun here and there."

You nod your head in agreement.

"But," Ann eyes Michelle knowingly, "there's probably something you'd like to change about your life."

You think for a moment and nod your head tentatively.

"Maybe you'd like a new career or a more satisfying relationship. Maybe you have a dream in the back of your mind — something you'd like to fulfill one day, but haven't gotten around to doing anything about."

"Maybe you've tried to make changes in your life," Michelle interjects, "like starting a new exercise routine or a diet."

"Umm-hmm."

"You may have talked to a girlfriend about wanting to get in shape. She listened, gave you some ideas, maybe even walked with you during your lunch hour."

"Umm-hmm."

"And that was helpful, but after a while you got bored or life got in the way. You stopped your exercise routine; you stopped eating healthy food." Michelle pauses and swigs the last of her orange juice. "Does this sound familiar?"

"Yep, sure does. So where is this going?"

"We're here to show you how to make those kinds of changes in your life stick," Ann asserts. "How to make your dreams a reality, how to achieve your goals."

You think to yourself: This sounds too good to be true.

Noting your cynical look, Ann asks, "This sounds too good to be true, right?"

Michelle nudges you and whispers, "Here's the part where an open mind really counts."

"We've found," continues Ann, "that women can achieve more of their goals by using the support of other women."

"Makes sense," you say, "but what's so special about that?"

"Great question!" replies Ann. "As you probably know, it's natural for women to support each other."

You nod, remembering the friends you've helped — and who've helped you — through the years.

"We've found that great things result when women get together to tell each other their goals, motivate each other to meet those goals, and hold each other accountable."

"Is that what the two of you do?"

"Yep, it sure is. We've been using the Goal Sister process for almost a decade. It's helped us immensely in achieving our personal and professional goals."

"How did all this start?"

"We met in 1993," answers Michelle, "when we both worked at a substance-abuse treatment agency in Bloomington, Illinois. I was a program evaluator in the research department, and Ann was a counselor. We quickly became friends when we realized that we shared similar interests and values — and a similar sense of humor. When I decided to leave the agency in 1995 to start my own program-evaluation business, I shared my fears and doubts with Ann — as well as my hopes and dreams. In addition to my husband, Bart, it was great to have Ann support me, listen to all the new things I was learning, and nudge me to keep moving forward."

"Then it was my turn," Ann chimes in. "Within a year of Michelle's leaving the agency, I felt a shift in my life. I'd been romantically involved with a man in Missouri, and I wanted more closeness in that relationship. I created a plan to leave both my job and the state of Illinois. Michelle helped me set goals and visualize my move to Missouri and the job that would take me there. Being able to give her a quick call or meet for an 'emergency' brainstorming session rejuvenated and refocused me."

"Little did Ann and I know that we were creating the Goal Sister process," adds Michelle. "We started writing down our goals and meeting weekly to review our progress, share resources, and encourage each other. After Ann moved to Joplin, Missouri, we adapted the process by meeting face-to-face every few months and using e-mail, instant messaging, and phone calls to maintain contact between meetings."

"Hmm, that's interesting," you reply. "And what kinds of success have you had?"

"Michelle started a consulting business, then ended it when she became employed part-time as an HIV/AIDS researcher on a national study," answers Ann. "She still works as a researcher while pursuing new writing opportunities. When she turned forty, Michelle started eating better and exercising daily. She had put off taking care of herself for many years, but she found the determination to lead a healthier life using the Goal Sister process. Another big success for Michelle and her family was moving from Illinois to Hawaii, where Michelle grew up, to live closer to her parents."

"You live in Hawaii, Michelle?"

"Yep! It's great being home again and having my children Zoë and Kanoa experience the rest of their childhood in Hawaii," Michelle responds. "And I'm not the only one who's had success using the Goal Sister process. Ann has made several career shifts and currently runs her own coaching and training business. She has written over one hundred articles, produced two booklets, and self-published a children's book. Ann has also let go of several activities and habits that no longer benefit her. She gave up a draining volunteer job at her church and focused her attention on deepening her spiritual faith. She stopped eating fast food and started exercising regularly. Ann has lost over fifty pounds! She's had nearly all her clothing altered to fit her new body."

Ann smiles and adds, "Michelle and I have also traveled together, pushed each other to live authentic lives, and gained greater clarity about what's important to us. We have an ongoing commitment that has brought us continuing success."

"Wow, you two have accomplished a lot together! You're really dedicated to working on your goals, aren't you?"

"We definitely are," replies Ann. "We want others to experience the kind of success we've had, and we're committed to sharing the process with as many women as possible."

"Which brings us back to you," Michelle interjects. "We're here today to share the Goal Sister process with you so that you can achieve your own personal and professional goals with a little help from your friends."

You sit up in your chair. "I'm interested! I want to hear more — like where do I find my Goal Sister?"

"That's in chapter 2," Ann replies.

"Chapter 2?"

"Of our book. We've written a book to show women all they need to know about finding and being a Goal Sister."

"What else does your book cover?"

"We're glad you asked," says Michelle. "Part 1 describes in detail what a Goal Sister is and how to start your Goal Sister friendship. You'll also learn how to get ready to be a Goal Sister, including how to prepare other people in your life for the process you're about to embark on."

Ann looks over at you and asks, "Still interested? Want a refill?"

"Yes — to both. Keep going, please."

"Okay," says Michelle, "We call part 2 'Living La Vida Goal Sister.' We describe in detail how to hold successful Goal Sister meetings, how to create and commit to achieving your goals, and how to motivate each other. We also have chapters in part 2 that show you how to handle your fears, doubts, and limiting beliefs. We use real-life examples from our own experience to show you how we achieved our goals and problem-solved difficult situations together."

"We placed the stories wherever they best illustrate the components of the process," adds Ann. "And, in addition to our own experiences, we include stories from the Goal Sister group we formed."

You perk up. "There's a group of Goal Sisters?"

"Yep," Ann smiles. "After eight years of success with the process, Michelle and I wanted to find out if it would work as well for other women. So in the spring of 2002, I tested the process for eight weeks by facilitating a group of seven Goal Sisters."

"We both learned a lot from that experience," notes Michelle. "We've included many of the group members' success stories in the book. The group was so successful that they didn't want to quit after eight weeks, so Ann still facilitates their monthly meetings."

"That's awesome! What else is in the book?"

"Part 3 starts with a chapter on taking overnight adventures with your Goal Sister," says Ann. "We encourage you and your Goal Sister to get away from your regular lives and have fun together while working on your goals. Michelle and I have held Goal Sister meetings at motels and at a friend's home. We bring along our favorite snack foods, drinks, and music, and we spend a productive, fun-filled day or two shopping, exercising, hanging out at bookstores, and eating out together. We laugh, we cry, and we get very pumped up about our goals. We talk about what's getting us stuck, what's working, new books we've found to help us get unstuck, new actions we're taking, new thoughts we're having. The possibilities are endless."

"That's when the Goal Sister process really gets cooking," Michelle interjects. "While you're having fun together, away from it all, many opportunities bubble up for you to delve into your stuff."

"Stuff? What stuff?"

"Lots of emotional things can come up. We call them 'limiting beliefs.' We spend quite a bit of time in chapter 7 helping you identify and reframe your limiting beliefs."

"This sounds a little like therapy."

"Well," responds Ann, "I'm a personal life coach and Michelle has a Ph.D. in clinical-community psychology, so no doubt this process reflects our training and experiences. But we purposely designed the Goal Sister process to focus on strengths, not weaknesses — to be forward-looking, not a way to analyze each other's childhood issues — and to help each other with solutions."

"Before you go any farther, Ann," adds Michelle, "I just want to make sure it's clear that we urge women who need professional counseling to get it. The Goal Sister process isn't meant to take the place of therapy. The process may help some women see that they would benefit from being in therapy, but Goal Sisters aren't therapists for each other."

"Okay, that makes sense," you say. "What else is in your book?"

"The rest of part 3 is full of examples of how to stay on track with your Goal Sister friendship," answers Ann. "We know it isn't always easy to work toward your goals, and we want you to be prepared for whatever comes your way. Then, in the last part of our book, we talk about a choice that you and your Goal Sister will face once you start achieving many of your goals: whether to continue together with the Goal Sister process. We've found that the answer depends on each woman and her unique situation. For some, it may be time to end the connection and go your separate ways or find another Goal Sister; for others, it may be time to intensify the connection and take it in a new direction."

"So, that's it," announces Michelle. "Did we forget anything?"

"Hmmm...we forgot to mention the exercises!" responds Ann. "We include exercises throughout the book that challenge you to reflect, to stretch from where you are now to where you want to be, and to take action. We encourage you to write down your thoughts and responses, and we strongly suggest you do so in a journal."

"We love our journals," declares Michelle. "They're also great for writing down our goals and keeping track of our own and each other's progress."

"So now that we've given you the highlights, what do you think?" asks Ann.

"I think I want to start reading chapter 1!"

"Yes!!" Ann and Michelle shout as they high-five you and each other.

Ann pulls a book out of her bag. "We were hoping you'd say that. And guess what? So was your friend; she bought you a copy of our book."

"She did? That's great! I can't wait to call her and thank her. Thank you both. This feels like the beginning of something so right for me."

"It is. Believe us, it is," Ann replies.

"Okay, girls," interrupts Michelle. "Let's put this food away and wash the dishes so that you can get started on the next chapter of your great life."

Part I

Embarking
on the Goal Sister Process

Chapter 1

The Enduring Gift of Female Friendship

We invite you to take a moment to remember your first childhood girlfriends. Were they neighbors or girls you met at school? Maybe you took swimming lessons together or your moms knew each other and introduced you. Maybe your best friend was your sister or a friend you got to know through Girl Scouts. Think of them now and silently thank them. For, without knowing it, they helped you form your ideas about the influence and power of female friendship, just as you did for them.

You probably remember discussing with your girlfriends all the unreasonable things grown-ups asked you to do: help with dishes, pull weeds, fold laundry, clean your room, and other such outrageous demands. You complained and resisted, knowing it was more fun to be outside playing with your friends, or at the movies or the mall with them. Your friends provided a window onto a new world of possibilities. You shared secrets with one another. Your girlfriends energized you, comforted you when you were down, and helped you forget about the tough spots in your life. They also celebrated your birthdays, the news of your first kiss, getting that date to the prom, and the team's championship season, among other highlights.

These early friends were what many of our favorite self-help authors call your "believe in you" people. They were willing to listen and encourage you, scream and cry with you, and see you through whatever drama you were having in math class, on the playground, or at home. They sought you out in the cafeteria, hung out with you after school, or called you every night. They shared your tastes in music. They supported whatever story you made up to tell your mom about where you were going, and they kept the secret destination just that: a secret. In short, they were the ones who believed that you could do anything and who knew that you deserved your successes.

Have Journal, Will Travel

As we mentioned in the introduction, we strongly encourage you to use a journal or notebook to record your goals and to write your responses to the exercises in this book. It doesn't have to be a new journal or notebook; it might be one you already started; it might be one you got for your birthday three years ago; it might be one you bought to record progress toward a goal, then only wrote in once or twice. But if you prefer, you can buy a brand-new journal or notebook to launch your Goal Sister process. If you prefer to type out your thoughts on a personal computer, that's okay — but it's not ideal. We recommend using a journal or notebook so that you can easily carry it to your Goal Sister meetings. But you know what works best for you!

Ann's Story

I've been blessed all my life with wonderful friends. Maybe it's because I'm an only child and needed to reach out to people to feel a sense of connection. No matter what the reason, I'm grateful for all the support I've had. Two childhood girlfriends come to mind when I think back. Lisa and Leigh saw me through those elementary years that were so important in my development.

It was Lisa who helped me through grade school when I was secretly scared to death to leave home and go to school. I would simply walk three blocks to Lisa's house every morning, and she would walk with me the rest of the way. I see now that her role in my life was to help me overcome fear. She had what I thought was a large dog, and I was scared of him. Even now I can see that dog's curious expression as if to say, "Why are you afraid of me? I'm harmless." And indeed he was. It took many months for me to be able to walk through Lisa's front door and pet her dog before she and I took off for school. On the way, we talked about everything under the sun. Twice a week, we stopped at the local candy store for a treat after school. That was my first lesson in recognizing that good things are even better when they're shared with someone.

Leigh lived in Virginia, which is where my dad's side of the family lives. We lived there for a few years while my dad was going through cancer treatment (he died when I was eight years old). I attended private school there, and Leigh was in my class. We became good friends. After my mom and I moved away, Leigh was the only one who stayed in touch, writing long letters to let me know that she missed me and still wanted my opinion on boys and clothes. That felt good! When my mom and I traveled back to Virginia every summer, I made sure I got to see Leigh. We had so much fun going to Virginia Beach and lurking around the Peppermint Beach Club — the area's then-biggest nightclub. That was tons of fun for us at age twelve! Our dreams included a summer romance that would find us dancing the night away at that club. It never happened, but Leigh was the first friend to tell me that it could. She was also the one to show me that, for those who are truly friends, there is no distance.

While I've lost contact with both Lisa and Leigh, my heart is still connected with theirs, and I'm grateful for their lasting influence on my life. Wherever you girls are, I wish you well!

Michelle's Story

When I was growing up, my best friends were my sisters, Renée and Laurie. We grew up in Hawaii, on the island of Oahu. I have many fond memories of times spent with my sisters, but one adventure stands out. I was seven years old, Renée was six, and Laurie was four. We were on a family trip to Kauai. After playing for a while in the hotel pool, we decided to head to the beach for more fun. Our adventure started when I spied a pile of plastic rafts on the beach. Not knowing any better, my sisters and I took one of them without permission and goofed around in the waves near the shore. Our mom was on the beach, reading her book. If we drifted too far from her spot, she would shout at us to move back toward her.

At some point, we started pretending to swim away from an imaginary monster. All three of us paddled playfully on the raft, laughing and chattering away. After a while, I peered down into the water and noticed how dark blue it had suddenly become. Looking up, I realized that we were at the mouth of the harbor, heading out to sea! I gasped and got my sisters' attention. We all gasped in unison, turned the raft around, and hung on for dear life as we paddled like crazy toward the beach. When I could finally touch the bottom again, I dragged the raft and my worn-out sisters back to shore. We lay on the sand, breathing heavily, not saying much to each other. Later, we talked about how we successfully outsmarted and out-swam our imaginary monster. We returned the plastic raft without our mom ever finding out how close we came to death!

Most of our adventures took place on our dead-end street. Playing kickball with the neighborhood kids, towing each other in our wagon with our bicycles, making tents out of old bedspreads and clothespins, helping each other with our chores, watching television after school; our time together cemented our connection as sisters. On one of my favorite episodes of The Brady Bunch, *Mrs. Brady and Marcia sing together:*

> Wherever we go, whatever we do,
> we're gonna go through it together!
> We may not go far, but sure as a star,
> wherever we are it's together!*

They were singing about me and my sisters. As we got through our silly and serious trials and tribulations together, we could always count on each other to be there with a "what are we doing for fun today?" attitude, a Band-Aid for our scrapes and cuts, and a stuffed animal for our woes and disappointments.

Exercise 1.1:
Who Were Your Childhood Girlfriends?

It's your turn now. Get out your journal and write down the names of three or more girlfriends you remember from childhood. Look at each name and reflect on the gifts they brought to your life. What did sharing life with them offer you? More excitement? More security about yourself? Did you learn about trust, creativity, loyalty? Perhaps your friendship offered you new and different experiences. Whatever the case, jot down your memories and reflections next to your childhood girlfriends' names.

---

* Lyrics from "Together Wherever We Go," originally from *Gypsy,* by Stephen Sondheim. Reprinted by permission.

As we grow up, we tend to measure our friends against that original picture of what a friend is. We all want a best friend who agrees with our views, tells us we're wonderful, and is available for fun at a moment's notice. You know who she is: She's the one who's heard about your good and bad days, who knows you inside and out. She's the friend you can't just casually say "hi" to; you have to stop what you're doing and share the details of your day. But while you may have a lot in common with this friend, sometimes it feels like she knows too much about you and your foibles. You might hesitate to tell her that you're starting a new exercise routine, because she might bring up all the exercise routines you've blown in the past five years! She may not be the first friend you think of when you're considering starting your own business; while she probably has your best interests at heart, she might question your choices and try to impose her values on you. Or she might judge you but hold back her true feelings because she doesn't want to upset you. She might even be jealous of your new ideas and successes. For many of us, she may not be the friend we need to support us through our changes right now. Enter a Goal Sister.

What Is a Goal Sister?

A Goal Sister is a blend of the best parts of your childhood and adult friends: a cherished confidante, buddy, cheerleader, muse, and guide. A Goal Sister is a woman who supports you to create and achieve your dreams and goals. Her values and beliefs are compatible with yours. She listens to your heart's desires and holds your vision. She takes a stand for you and your goals. She helps you start with the end in sight and work backward to identify the steps to take toward that end. She provides suggestions on how to make your goals become your reality. A Goal Sister gives you honest feedback about how your desires may be received by others, then assists you in accomplishing them anyway. She validates your feelings, inspires you, and offers a different perspective on situations that may bog down your progress. A Goal Sister gently challenges you and holds you accountable for creating the very best life you can imagine. And she trusts that you can do it, in spite of and in conjunction with all the other demands you have on your time.

A Goal Sister helps you achieve the goals and dreams you have for all areas of your life, not just work, parenting, or health. She knows that you want to do your best in all ways, not just a few. A Goal Sister looks at the big picture and asks you hard questions to determine where your priorities lie and how balance can be brought to all of them. But a Goal Sister isn't connected to every aspect of your life; you needn't put a lot of energy into your Goal Sister friendship, because the boundaries of your relationship are clearly defined and respected.

Goal Sisters come from diverse backgrounds: Some are single, some are mothers, some are grandmothers, some live near family members, some live alone. Goal Sisters have diverse life experiences: Some are artists, some clean houses for a living, some are students, some are teachers, some are retired, some work for big companies, some work out of their homes, some work with their hands for a living, some work with their heads for a living. Goal Sisters yearn to achieve different professional and personal dreams: Some want to change careers, some want to lose twenty pounds, some want to be closer with their partners, some want to do more of the things they love, some want less stress in their lives. Some want to make small changes, and others want to take giant leaps.

Michelle's Story

Back in 1993, I was in desperate need of a Goal Sister. I was a happily married working mom, with two children under four years old. My job of two years as a program evaluator at a substance-abuse treatment agency in Bloomington, Illinois, was starting to wear on me. I spent too many hours each week away from my family; my department wasn't heading in a direction that fit with my interests; and my morale was at an all-time low. That's when I began exploring the option of starting my own program-evaluation business.

I didn't know anyone who had taken this kind of leap, so I began to educate myself about the necessary steps. I quickly became overwhelmed with all the information I had to digest and the decisions I had to make. My husband, Bart, was very supportive of my explorations, and he listened to me jabber on about newfound business books and ideas. My best friend, Tomas, was also supportive, even though my departure from the agency would affect my ability to evaluate his Chicago-based HIV/AIDS mental-health project. My small circle of female friends also encouraged my new exploration.

But something — or more like someone — was missing from my network of support. I yearned to talk with someone who shared a history with me and who accepted me "as is." My sisters, Renée and Laurie, obviously came to mind, but they lived in California and were busy with raising their own children. I wanted to share my progress and setbacks with someone who knew that I was crazy to want to leave such a secure, well-paying job — but who would encourage me to do it anyway. Bart, Tomas, and a few girlfriends fit this category, but they didn't meet another important criterion: someone who had nothing to gain or lose from my starting my own business. The only one left standing was Ann.

I would be lying if I told you that I figured this out in one afternoon. What really happened is that, over the course of a year of talking about my plans with supportive family and friends, Ann emerged as my new Goal Sister. She understood my frustrations with my current job, she was available to meet with me in person, she gave me helpful resources and leads, she encouraged me to think and act big, and she helped me set and achieve my goals. By the time I left the agency in 1995, I had a new part-time job in Champaign, Illinois, that allowed me the flexibility to run my own program-evaluation business and pursue additional consulting opportunities. I was able to continue working on Tomas's evaluation project and write grants with him for new projects. And my newly formed connection with Ann became the beginning of a lasting Goal Sister friendship.

What a Goal Sister Is Not

- MALE BASHER: Goal Sisters don't get together to talk about the men in our lives, unless it's about how supportive they are of our goals. Our focus is on us and on helping each other achieve our goals!

- GOSSIPMONGER: Similarly, Goal Sisters don't spend their valuable time together gossiping about the latest goings-on at the office or in the PTA. We have more constructive things to do.

- CRITIC: If you're like us, you probably already have a critic who lives in your head. She's the part of you that doesn't believe in you and your abilities. We actively discourage our Goal Sister from joining forces with our critics.

- AGENT: While your Goal Sister may be your biggest fan, she's not responsible for promoting you and your dreams. You are! Your Goal Sister can help you generate ideas about who else might help you in those efforts.

- PARTY PAL: It's true that Goal Sisters like to have fun. We enjoy listening to music, dancing, and flirting like any other social butterfly. But we'd rather meet to discuss our goals at a bookstore than a bar; it might be difficult to chat about personal aspirations over the background noise in the bar.

- THERAPIST: Working on your goals can sometimes bring up issues that are beyond the scope of a Goal Sister friendship. If that happens, we encourage you to respect the boundaries of your friendship and get the help you need from a therapist.

Key Ingredients of the Goal Sister Process

Is it just us, or does everyone's mom have a special recipe for meat-loaf? What makes your mom's recipe special? Ann's mom added Ritz crackers and ketchup for extra flavor; Michelle's mom includes wheat germ, shredded carrots, chopped celery, and an egg. Like our moms' recipes for meatloaf, there isn't anything orig-inal or particularly different about the key ingredients of the Goal Sister process; what makes it unique is how the ingredients are combined and used by women interested in making lasting changes in their lives. Here are the five key ingredients that make the Goal Sister process comforting yet unusual:

1. Support

Flip through any women's fitness magazine, and you're bound to find an article that describes how women accomplish their fitness goals using a buddy system. Giving and receiving ongoing support with your Goal Sister can help you accomplish more than just fitness goals; it also works well for spiritual goals, creativity goals, relationship goals, and others. We're talking about emotional, physical, social, and problem-solving support. Being supportive can range from telling your Goal Sister, "I believe in you," when she's nervous about making a presentation in front of a large audi-ence, to sending her a card letting her know you'll be with her "in spirit" when she's going through a difficult breakup with her part-ner, to helping her paint a few walls in her house before she puts it up for sale. It may be a cliché, but our Goal Sister Motto works: Helping You Helps Me!

2. Motivation

As women, we're accustomed to cheering on our children, our best friends, and anyone we care about; it comes naturally to most of us. Goal Sisters motivate each other to take the first step, the sec-ond step, even the two-hundredth step toward achieving their goals. Most people lapse here and there after making changes in their lives. It's hard to stay motivated on your own, and it can be very hard to stick to new routines and lifestyles. That's where your Goal Sister comes in. She might motivate you by saying, "You can do it!" when you need an extra boost to meet your writing dead-line, or by sending you healthy recipes when you're trying to cut back on fatty foods, or by creating a sticker chart to help you to track the days when you practice a hobby you'd like to get better at. There are endless ways for you and your Goal Sister to keep each other motivated and on track with your goals.

3. Accountability

Despite a desire to set and attain goals, many women never initi-ate change, while others slip back into old feelings and behaviors before making any significant changes. There are many reasons why this happens. Sometimes the changes you make don't stick because your new routine becomes boring. Sometimes your signi-ficant others, family, or friends may try to bring you back to the old status quo when your progress threatens your relation-ships with them. You may even begin to doubt yourself. Your Goal Sister can keep you accountable to your goals by using gentle nudges ("How are you coming with drinking eight glasses of water a day?"), pointed questions ("If you want to start your morn-ings with a five-minute meditation, why did you just agree to carpool the kids to the 6:00 A.M. swimming class?"), or piercing zaps ("Actions speak louder than words!"). Keeping each other accountable can be tricky; we've dedicated sections of chapter 8 to showing you how to master this part of the Goal Sister process.

Ann and Michelle's Story

Joan was the assistant manager of our favorite gift shop in the Lakeview neighborhood of Chicago. One day as we shopped, she overheard us talking about our goals and asked us if we did this all the time. Ann said, "Yes, we do. So tell us, what's your *dream? What would you rather be doing than working in retail?" "My dream," Joan answered, "is to be the head librarian at a university library. Actually, that was my dream until I realized after getting my degree how hard it would be to get that job without the right connections." She shrugged her shoulders and said, "I gave up trying, and here I am."*

Joan talked about making enough money to support herself and her cat, to take weekend trips to Wisconsin, and to buy books. "I have stacks of books everywhere!" She talked about loving mysteries, science fiction, and poetry. "I use to love self-help books," she said, "but I've given up reading them because they haven't helped me much." When Michelle asked her why, Joan described how she'd get excited about a new weight-loss book, start reading it, do the exercises, then quit within two weeks because she got bored or lost her motivation. "Plus, I didn't see any results." That wasn't the only kind of self-help program Joan had started and stopped. She also talked about having read books to figure out why she kept falling for the wrong guys. "Those books were interesting, but they didn't really help me. My love life is either a mess or non-existent."

Then Ann asked her, "Besides reading books, what makes you really happy?" Joan's face lit up and she said, "Playing my guitar. My favorite place to hang out is the Old Town School of Music. I wish I were good enough to play guitar there." Then Ann asked Joan what three steps she could take to play guitar for a living at the Old Town School of Music. Joan paused and answered, "I know the manager there. I could tell him that I'm interested in opening for one of the shows and see what he says. In the meantime, I could play my guitar on open mike night at the bar around the corner from my place. I could also spend more time after work jamming with my musician friends, and I could ask them what it takes to make it full-time." Michelle mentioned that Joan had obviously thought this through. "Oh yeah, sure I have," *said Joan,* "I *think about it all the time. I just haven't done anything about it. I guess I'm scared to leave this job, and I don't have a good track record with making changes in my life."*

That's when we told Joan about Goal Sisters, and how she could use the process to realize her dream of playing the guitar professionally — and, at some point, to lose weight and improve her love life. "You mean, someone would ask me how I'm doing with my goals? And she would be there if I needed support? And I could tell her where I'm getting stuck, and she would help me work through it? Sign me up!" *We suspect Joan has found her Goal Sister by now, and that she'll be playing at a major gig sometime soon.*

4. Interest and Investment

Sometimes it's awkward to talk about the kinds of changes we'd like to make in our lives or how we're going about making those changes. For example, it's not always easy to tell others that you want more meaning in your life or to share your experiences with trying a new self-help program. That's not the kind of conversation we typically have with others over coffee or during the halftime show of a football game. Often, we hesitate to share our dreams with others because we're afraid of their reactions. "What if they think I'm ridiculous? What if they laugh?" When you share your dreams with your Goal Sister, she'll ask you to tell her more about them and why achieving them matters so much. She'll do so without judgment and preconceived notions about your abilities and your level of commitment. That's one of her gifts to you: caring about your goals and being invested in helping you achieve them.

5. Fun and Focus

Many self-help authors discourage their readers from having fun while setting and attaining goals. We understand where that mindset comes from; we grew up hearing many messages about keeping work and play separate. We also live in a culture that promotes the image of the independent woman who is forging ahead for higher status and pay in order to have more possessions. While this may be a popular image, it doesn't help those of us who want to balance it all while improving ourselves. We believe that you can do just that. Goal Sisters can have fun while staying focused on achieving their goals. For example, you and your Goal Sister can hold a meeting at a neighborhood pool and swim around while talking about your health goals. You and your Goal Sister can write goals in each other's journals using different colored markers that correspond with different categories. Keeping fun in the mix helps make the goal-setting process less cumbersome!

Benefits of the Goal Sister Process

There are many benefits of the Goal Sister process. The most apparent is that two heads and hearts are better than one when it comes to achieving goals. Other benefits of the Goal Sister process are:

Ongoing In-Person Contact

When you're struggling with your fears about making changes, nothing can replace ongoing face-to-face contact with someone who's invested in your success and may have been in your shoes. Having the opportunity to know your Goal Sister personally, to pick your Goal Sister's brains, and to learn from her experiences can give you insight and courage to face your doubts and fears.

Ann's Story

My move from Bloomington, Illinois, to Joplin, Missouri, in 1997 was the right thing for me to do, both personally and professionally. I enjoyed my second job in Missouri, as a substance abuse counselor for teens, but after a couple of years, I was uncomfortable with the scheduled hours. I had a tough time making the decision to leave this job because I enjoyed my coworkers and I believed in the work we were doing. But I was intent on devoting myself full-time to life coaching and training. As I wrestled with my fears and doubts, Michelle was there to say, "Do it! Take the leap!"

It was good to have Michelle there for me. Indeed, she mirrored the role I had played for her when she left her job at the substance-abuse agency years before. I know she appreciated the support I gave her then; it amuses me now that I could do it so easily for her, but struggled with my own decision. Isn't that usually the way it goes? We see clearly the path for someone else, but we allow doubts and fears to take control of our own similar situation.

I left that job in 2001. Throughout the process of leaving my job and adjusting to my new routine, it helped to have Michelle's constant reminder that I could succeed. It took me a while to find my rhythm and flow. I appreciated Michelle's balanced support; she didn't push me any more than I was ready to be pushed, yet she managed to convey her belief in me and her support of my business plan. It takes a special friend to provide that kind of unconditional encouragement. As Goal Sisters, we have learned the delicate dance of supporting and nudging.

Help in Maintaining Your Success

As avid readers of self-help books, we've noticed that many of the current books on setting and achieving goals give minimal attention to helping readers maintain their gains. Maintaining your goal achievements is an important part of the Goal Sister process; a section of chapter 10 is dedicated to showing you how that's done.

An Adjunct to Other Self-Help Programs

We know from personal and professional experience that it's impossible for any single self-help program to fit every woman's

needs and situation. It's more likely that different self-help programs speak to different parts of women and at different times in
their lives. Knowing this, we encourage women to find new (or
rediscover old) self-help programs that resonate with them, and to
use the Goal Sister process to make their resulting new thoughts,
feelings, or behaviors into new habits.

Michelle's Story

*When my children were very young, I had few friends to talk
with about making changes in my life. The reality was that
I didn't have time for friends. After toiling at my desk for
eight hours, and being a mom before and after work, I was
exhausted by the end of the day. If I had spare time in the
evenings, I'd do chores or vegetate in front of the television
with my husband. I could have talked with some of my female
coworkers who were in similar situations, but I wasn't comfortable doing that because all we seemed to have in common
was our place of employment.*

*What I really wanted was a friend who was a working
mom — someone who had figured out how to have it all and
keep her life in balance. I didn't find that friend at work, so I
looked to self-help books for the answers. And boy, did I find
some great books! I cannot tell you how many times I wanted to
contact the authors and say, "You really nailed this issue on the
head! Thank you, thank you for letting me know that I'm not
alone," or ask them for support around dealing with a problem
they seemed to relate to. But those self-help authors weren't
around to talk to, so I underlined meaningful passages in my
books, drew lightbulbs next to paragraphs that gave me special
insight, and dreamed of someday sharing my thoughts and feelings with someone who understood what I was going through.*

*That day didn't come until we expanded the Goal Sister
process and started meeting regularly with a mutual friend
named Faith. Faith worked at the substance-abuse treatment*

agency where Ann and I worked. The three of us met as Goal Sisters for about two years, primarily to focus on our business goals. When Ann moved to Missouri in 1997, Faith and I continued to meet every few months. Like me, Faith was married, worked full-time, and had children. Her children were older than mine, which was an advantage in my eyes because she had lived through what I was still struggling with. Faith's experiences — and the way she helped me feel normal — relieved some of my guilt about being a working mother. We even talked about how the guilt never completely goes away. Her experience provided me with a much-needed touchstone for my new perspectives and actions — changes I was making thanks to the self-help books I'd read. For both Ann and me, Faith's presence was an important part of laying the groundwork for the Goal Sister process.

A Ripple Effect That Enhances Your Other Bonds

A synergy is created when you truly commit to the Goal Sister process with someone who's as dedicated to your success as you are to hers. Conversations become more real and direct. You develop more compassion and honesty. Your mind opens to the area "outside the box" instead of just the old, familiar ways. Your other relationships may be influenced by this synergy and begin to change as well. You might develop more realistic expectations of your significant other's role in your life. You might be inspired to revive a stale relationship. You might gain greater clarity around your wants and needs in your friendships. This is usually for the better, though we must admit that we ended some friendships that continually derailed us from focusing on the direction and support we wanted in our lives.

Sharing the Success

After eight years of success with the Goal Sister process, we wanted to share it with others. So we designed eight sessions to involve a

group of women in the Goal Sister process. Here is the story of
how the first Goal Sister group came to be.

Goal Sister Group Story

*Ann offered to facilitate the eight-week Goal Sister pilot pro-
gram in her home in Joplin. A month before the first planned
meeting, Ann began to spread the word about the group to
people in her personal and professional network. In a few
weeks, her phone started to ring; in March of 2002, eight
women arrived at Ann's home for the first meeting. Michelle
was there, too; she drove eight hours from her home in Illinois
to participate in the first group meeting.*

*There was a lot of anticipation and uneasiness in the air
that first night. Ann shared her intentions for the group while
Michelle passed out written materials describing the Goal Sister process. Ann asked each woman to introduce herself, tell
why she was there, and share her expectations.*

*Arlene wanted to write more. MJ wanted to get over a
difficult divorce and move on with her life. Nelda was tired
of being told by her friends and family that there was no need
to strive for anything more in her life. Joy was concerned that
the group might be a pyramid scheme, and that the members
would be asked to pay hundreds of dollars for the secret to a
great life. Cindy said that years of putting others' needs before
her own had stymied her emotions and forced her to put her
goals on hold. Karen had enjoyed attending another group led
by Ann and felt that she could benefit from further contact
with her. Deborah wasn't sure why she was there or what she
hoped to get from participating.*

*At the end of the first meeting, every woman made a com-
mitment to get together for another seven weeks. Each one
stated a goal and identified an obstacle that was holding her
back. They all exchanged phone numbers and decided who*

would provide snacks at the next meeting. They were well on their way.

Although the Goal Sister group was intended as an eight-week program to test the principles and exercises in this book, it was so successful that the members still meet monthly. You'll get to know them throughout this book, and you'll probably recognize yourself in some of their stories. You may find that they have similar concerns, similar challenges, and the same inner voice that asks, "Why not now?" The difference is that the Goal Sister group members have found each other, while you still need to identify your potential Goal Sisters. You're in luck; we'll show you how to do that in the next chapter.

Chapter 1 Summary

★ Your childhood girlfriends helped you form your ideas about the power of female friendship, just as you did for them. They believed that you could do anything, and they knew that you deserved your successes.

★ As you grew up, you might have sought the support of your best friend as your life changed. She might have agreed with your views and told you that you're wonderful. But, for many reasons, your best friend may not be the one you need to support you in reaching your goals right now. Enter a Goal Sister!

★ A Goal Sister is a blend of the best parts of your childhood and adult friends: cherished confidante, buddy, cheerleader, muse, and guide. Her values and beliefs are compatible with yours. She listens to your heart's desires and believes in your vision. She helps you achieve your goals in every area of your life.

★ The five key ingredients of the Goal Sister process are:

1. Goal Sisters give and receive ongoing emotional, information-sharing, and problem-solving **support**;

2. Goal Sisters **motivate** each other to take the first step, the second step, and even the two-hundredth step toward achieving their goals;

3. Goal Sisters use a variety of **accountability** strategies, including gentle nudges and pointed questions;

4. Goal Sisters have mutual **interest and investment** in each other's success; and

5. Goal Sisters incorporate **fun and focus** in their interactions.

★ The Goal Sister process is invaluable because:

• it gives you ongoing, in-person contact with someone who supports you in achieving your goals;

• it can serve as an adjunct to other self-help programs;

• it helps you maintain the success you've had in achieving your goals; and

• it enhances your other relationships.

Questions

★ *How can you benefit from having a Goal Sister support you in your life today?*

★ *What kinds of interaction do you want to bring from your childhood friendships into your new Goal Sister friendship?*

Chapter 2

Identifying and Approaching Your Goal Sister

Now that you know what a Goal Sister is and how much zip she can add to helping you change your life, it's time to talk about who she might be and what qualities will attract you to your potential Goal Sister. What path should you take to find her? Is she your best friend? Do you have to be from similar backgrounds or share certain life experiences? What if you're thinking of two or more women as potential Goal Sisters? So many questions! Fortunately, we have the answers.

Many Paths to Your Goal Sister

There is no single path to identifying your potential Goal Sisters. We've found Goal Sisters at our workplace, online, and by facilitating a group of women interested in working on their goals. Your situation will determine the many possible paths to your Goal Sister. This is the time to stay open and be aware of your interactions and connections with others as you begin your Goal Sister journey.

In-Person Connections

If you interact with women in your daily life, start there. Your potential Goal Sister is probably someone you already know. She may be someone who encourages you through compliments or thoughtful gestures. She may be someone who's caught your attention with her actions or her words.

We'll begin by telling you how we were drawn to each other as Goal Sisters. Each of us was attracted to the other for different reasons.

Michelle's Story

Ann counseled teens and adults on the other side of the building at the substance-abuse treatment agency where we both worked. Our paths didn't cross until she volunteered to join a committee that I started with a friend. Once a month, in a stuffy, dimly lit conference room, Ann and I — and a small gaggle of other women interested in recycling office paper — met over sandwiches, carrot sticks, chips, and apple slices to talk "trash."

That's when I started noticing certain qualities about Ann. She smiled a lot, laughed easily, and was always "on" — whether with ideas or with quick comebacks. I noticed that Ann knew every person in the agency. She couldn't go anywhere without someone thanking her for something she'd done for a client, or saying, "Hey, Ann, when you get a chance, can we talk?"

I learned that Ann was a mover and a shaker. She started the World AIDS Day event at our agency, and she got people who I thought would never participate to wear red ribbons, hang black crepe paper on artwork, and attend vigils.

People were always hanging out in Ann's office. She had the best toys: puppets, Silly Putty, magic wands. She had interesting stuff on her desk, including a bowl of condoms for her role as an HIV-prevention specialist.

Ann definitely caught my attention; she was someone I wanted to get to know better.

Ann's Story

People often ask me how I knew that Michelle and I would be good Goal Sisters. What signs did I look for in her? On what did I base my decision to share more of my life with her? I have to tell you that, when I look back on it, I can't recall a moment when I said, "Oh wow! She just showed me that it would be great to share goals with her!" Instead, it was more of a sense of knowing that I felt inside.

Yes, Michelle was a hard worker, and people seemed to rely on her for a lot of information and support. Yes, she was proud of her family and committed to her children. Yes, she had a fun office, complete with a LARGE plaster bust of Elvis Presley and colorful pictures that let me see her artistic side. These were all things I noticed and observed in my first few meetings with her.

I guess my real clue came when I heard Michelle's intentions and felt them resonate with mine. She wanted something more in her life; so did I. She knew that what she had was fine: bills were being paid, she was part of a successful research team within the agency, and she was well thought of by her clients. Yet Michelle was open to hearing the call to do something more with her life. I suspect she felt that similarity with me, too.

I was one of the first to learn of Michelle's plans to leave the agency where we worked. As she shared her dream of starting her own program-evaluation business, I remember thinking, "This woman thinks big like I do. She's not afraid to go out and get what she wants!" I could see her enthusiasm, and I heard her solid plan for action. I wanted to be around that kind of energy, and I knew we would probably provide good support for each other. As it turned out, I was right.

Your potential Goal Sister may be a member of a group you belong to. Or maybe you have a favorite chum or two you meet with regularly, whether they're former sorority sisters, other hobby enthusiasts, or members of a local business organization. You might begin to look at one of these old friends in a new light: Does her approach complement yours? Does she inspire you to stretch yourself or your thinking? Do you admire her infectious "can-do" attitude?

The story of the first Goal Sister group illustrates how a disparate group of women can come together and form new connections that turn them into Goal Sisters.

The Goal Sister Group Story

Many of the original Goal Sister group members knew Ann personally, but most of them didn't know each other very well at first. Ann knew MJ and Deborah through a magazine she wrote for. Arlene was a coworker in Ann's previous job as a counselor. Earlier in 2002, Ann had run a group that focused on accomplishing New Year's resolutions; Karen had been in that group and wanted to know if Ann had any other groups in the works. Karen brought Nelda and Cindy, friends of hers from work, and Cindy invited her friend, Joy. They all came to explore the possibility of having more in their lives.

What about you? Who do you know who could be your Goal Sister? As it was for us, she might be someone you work with or someone you serve with on a committee. She might be someone you go to movies, art galleries, or sporting events with. She might be someone you exercise with or someone you volunteer with.

Your Goal Sister might be a member of your prayer group, church, temple, or synagogue. She might be someone you know from a club you belong to or a class you take. She might be your neighbor or someone you commute with. She might be someone you met through your children or another family member. She might be someone in the community you admire, with whom you've had brief but positive interactions.

She might be someone you've known for a long time. You might have attended school together. She might be your best friend.

Exercise 2.1: Who Catches Your Attention?

For the next couple of days, notice the women you talk with, hang out with, or take a break from your day with. Who do you eagerly share good news with? Notice which women take the time to share their triumphs with you. Notice who you go to when you have a problem to solve. Notice how you feel when you're interacting with these women. Do they drain you or energize you? Do your interactions make you want to form a stronger connection with them? Write about your experiences in your journal.

Online Connections

If you don't have much contact with women in your daily life, the path to your potential Goal Sister may involve the Internet. Perhaps you're on an e-mail list with women who share your personal or professional interests. You may have noticed someone's postings and felt similarly about an issue. Maybe you take part in an online support group for women who are going through similar experiences, like being depressed or getting used to parenting a teenager. Although it's not the ideal way to interact with a Goal Sister, your online female friendships could lead you to your Goal Sister relationship.

Ann's Story

It is possible to forge a Goal Sister relationship with someone you haven't met. I had that experience in 2001, when I participated

in a twenty-eight-day online discussion group. I wanted to fol-
low their prescribed marketing plan for my coaching business.
The program offered an e-mail support list, and I signed up for
it. I noticed a message from a creative spirit who was seeking a
buddy for the program. MaryLu was from Chicago, a place I
was familiar with, and in graphic arts, a field that I felt would
match my creative streak. We exchanged e-mails about our
backgrounds and business goals. We found several similarities in
how we worked and in the experiences we'd been through. We
agreed to support each other in this process.

MaryLu and I identified the goals we wanted to attain in
each week of the twenty-eight-day program, and we set up a weekly
phone call to share our progress. It worked! We both noticed a dif-
ference in how well we met our goals, and we felt more motivated
to do so when we knew that our weekly phone call was coming up.

As we went through our second twenty-eight-day cycle,
we started talking about other areas of our lives. MaryLu then
helped me end a relationship and pursue writing this book.
She even served as a reader of our book proposal. I helped her
narrow her business niche and introduced her to elements of
coaching that she could utilize in her business.

MaryLu and I met in person when I attended a coach-
ing conference in Chicago. She was just as terrific in person as
she'd been on the phone and in e-mail. We still occasionally
e-mail each other. I know she'll be the first in line at our
Chicago-area book signing!

Extra Nudging

If you're having trouble coming up with possible Goal Sisters, we suggest that you review a list of the people in your
life. That information may be in an address book, an electronic organizer, or a computer database. Wherever you keep
this information, scan it to find names of potential Goal Sisters and write them in your journal.

Are You My Goal Sister?

Whether you know your potential Goal Sister in person or find her online, we believe there are certain qualities that a Goal Sister should possess. We're going to help you narrow your options using these qualities — and we'll have a little fun at the same time.

Exercise 2.2: Here She Comes, Ms. Goal Sister!

Imagine that a Goal Sister Ball is held in your honor. All the women on your list and all the other supportive people in your life are there. Everyone is dressed to the nines, eating their favorite food, drinking bubbly, and chattering excitedly or dancing to their favorite tunes.

The lights dim. You make a grand entrance in a splendid gown, with both of us accompanying you. We all approach the microphone. Everyone stops what they're doing to greet you with hearty claps, whistles, and "woo-hoos."

Ann welcomes your guests and announces, "We're here tonight to support our lovely hostess in choosing a Goal Sister." We both turn to you and smile. Ann faces the women seated on the stage and continues, "Congratulations to all of you for making her list of potential Goal Sisters. You're a special group."

After the applause quiets down, Michelle directs her gaze to your seated friends and says, "Our hostess is now going to answer eleven questions about each of you to help narrow her list of Goal Sister finalists." Several women onstage gasp and a hush falls over the crowd. Ann passes you a clipboard and pen while Michelle continues, "If you're not selected, please join us in wishing our hostess the best in choosing her Goal Sister, and stop by the reception in the banquet room afterward."

The spotlight shines on you, and you start to ask yourself the following questions about each of the women remaining onstage:

1. Is she fun to relate to?

2. Do I look forward to interacting with her?

3. Do I respect her views and the way she expresses herself?

4. Does interacting with her energize me?

5. Do our interactions bring out the best in me and in her?

6. Does she have time, or would she make time, to be my Goal Sister?

7. Does she have an open mind about trying new ideas?

8. Would I feel comfortable sharing my dreams with her?

9. Would she help me move forward instead of holding me back?

10. Do the qualities I admire in her complement my strengths and resources?

11. Is it possible to get together with her in person at least once every three months?

If you answer "no" to any of these questions, cross that woman's name off your list. Take a moment to appreciate what she brings to your life as she graciously leaves the stage. After you go through your entire list, you're likely to have one or more women remaining who scored a perfect eleven. They're seated in front of us, wondering what's going to happen next.

Ann steps back into the light and says, "Congratulations! You're all Goal Sister finalists." We all clap happily together. "Please remain seated and turn your attention once again toward our hostess, who's going to tell you about the goals she'd like to accomplish this next year."

You put down your clipboard and pen as you start describing some of the changes you'd like to make. While you're doing this, you notice the reactions of the remaining women. Which ones are nodding enthusiastically? Which ones are checking for messages on their cell phones and not really listening? Which ones are leaning forward in their chairs, excited by what you're saying? Which ones exude the passion you feel for your goals? You pick up your clipboard and pen, then you go over the eleven questions again with each of the remaining women.

After some time, you signal that you're ready to make your announcement, and you step up to the microphone. "I want you all to know that I've made my decision," you declare. "I'd like _____ to be my Goal Sister." You hear a squeal, and your new Goal Sister rushes up to you. As you embrace, she whispers, "Let's meet Friday at 12:00. You can tell me more then!" You feel great about your decision, knowing that your chosen Goal Sister is a woman of action, and that this new connection is the beginning of many possibilities for both of you.

Michelle announces: "You're all invited to join our hostess and her new Goal Sister in the banquet room to honor their commitment to the Goal Sister process." As you leave the stage and walk toward the banquet room, several supportive people in your life congratulate you and shout, "Way to go!" and "You go, girl!" One woman hugs you and says, "I'm still here for you if you need anything." Another group of women tell you that they want to periodically hear how you're doing with your health goals. A male friend asks, "We're still meeting at the park tomorrow with our kids, right?" You assure all of them that your friendship will continue, and you suggest that your female friends might find their own Goal Sisters in this group. Some women nod and glance around at each other; you see connections being made throughout the room.

What If Two or More Goal Sisters Make My Final List?

If more than one potential Goal Sister makes your final list, you might consider having two or three Goal Sisters. There are certainly benefits to going that route: You'll have more women to hold your vision, more women to share their experiences with you, and a variety of feedback and ideas that you probably wouldn't have received from just one person.

On the other hand, having several Goal Sisters might make it more difficult to schedule meeting times that everyone can attend. If one person misses a meeting, it will take longer to bring her up to speed on everyone's progress at the next meeting and to hear how she's doing with her goals. Meetings will take longer because there will be more people who need time to share their progress and their requests for support.

You'll have to weigh these pros and cons in making your final decision.

Making the Connection

Congratulations! You've made the first step toward committing to the Goal Sister process. You've given thought to the women in your life who inspire and motivate you. You've compiled a list of possible Goal Sisters and narrowed the search considerably. Now it's time to make the connection with the woman you've chosen, requesting her partnership on the road to your success — and hers.

How will you present the idea of having a Goal Sister to her? Will you give her a call or send her a card? Maybe you'll send her a quick e-mail letting her know you have a big project to discuss (after all, isn't your future a big project?). Getting clear about how to describe the process may be your first step.

Exercise 2.3: How Do You Define a Goal Sister?

Take only ten minutes to complete the following sentences in your journal:

1. For me, a Goal Sister is:

2. I am asking my Goal Sister for:

3. In return, I will give:

Review your completed statements, then take another five minutes to add to any of your responses.

How will you let your potential Goal Sister know that this is a serious commitment for you and not just another excuse to get together for coffee and catch up on all the news? Your tone and words will show her. Getting clearer about your expectations and what you're willing to give in return will help you to better express your request. You might also consider telling her why you selected her, for example: "I admire your perseverance," "I notice that you're very focused on what you want and seem to set manageable steps for yourself to get there," and "I think we have similar personalities and are both willing to work hard for what we want." Review your journal pages to jog your memory about the qualities you noticed about her.

So there you go! You know what you want, and you're ready to ask for a commitment from her. Go ahead: Make that call; send that note or e-mail. If she's interested (and most women will be), decide on where and when to meet. For our first meeting, we met at a restaurant close to where we worked so that we didn't have to spend too much time driving. We also met where there was easy parking and a short wait for a table. We recommend setting aside at least an hour for your first meeting. If you haven't talked with each other much about your life and the areas you'd like to improve, we suggest that you aim for an hour-and-a-half get-together.

First Encounter

During your first meeting, you'll want to describe what a Goal Sister is and the key elements of the Goal Sister process. Don't forget to bring your copy of this book! Let your Goal Sister know again why you thought she'd be great in this role. Tell her the story of how we became Goal Sisters.

Using the notes from your journal, tell her about your goals and the kind of support you'd like to receive in meeting them. Ask her about her goals, what kind of support she'd like to receive, and how much support she can provide. Listen to how she talks about her own life and what she's happy or unhappy with. Pay attention to how she responds to you: Is she excited for you? Encouraging? Interested? Does talking about your goals seem to motivate her to think more about hers?

Assess her level of commitment to changing her life and her readiness for change. How does she talk about her goals? Does she whine or complain a lot? How often does she use the "Yes, but..." excuse? How has she tried to work toward her goals in the past? Find out about her level of interest, commitment, and availability to do this *now;* does she have time to fit the Goal Sister process into her schedule?

Before your time together is over, ask if she's interested in being your Goal Sister. If she declines, then chalk one up for experience. If she's interested, exchange e-mail addresses and phone numbers (if you don't already have this information) and encourage her to think more about your request over the next week.

Is She the One?

Over the next week, carve out some quiet time for yourself and sit down with your journal to review your interaction with your potential Goal Sister. Did you leave your meeting feeling energized and enthusiastic about forming a new connection with her? Can you see yourself forming a partnership to help each other work toward your goals? Have you had any contact with each other since you met? If so, does she still sound interested? What does your gut say? Do you feel that you share enough similar values to make this work? Can she realistically make space in her life to do this? Write your responses to these questions in your journal.

If, after some thought, you feel that she's not the one, we suggest that you go back to your short list of women and figure out who to approach next. Try not to get frustrated; choosing the right Goal Sister is an important part of succeeding with this process. It's better to take the time to find someone who fits with what you need — and what you can offer her — than to settle for someone who isn't quite right.

If you decide that she's the one, contact her and ask if she feels the same way. If it's a go, congratulations! You're on your way to forming a friendship that will help you live a more successful, contented, fulfilled life.

You can have more of what you want in your life. As you and your Goal Sister move forward together, you'll be more and more convinced that this is true.

Chapter 2 Summary

★ There are many paths to finding your Goal Sister, including in-person and online connections. Be aware of who catches your attention during your daily life. Is it a woman you work with or attend organizational meetings with? Is she goal-oriented and ready to take the steps to reach her goals?

★ Whether you know your potential Goal Sister in person or find her online, there are certain qualities that she should possess. For each of your potential Goal Sisters, ask yourself:

- Is she fun to relate to?
- Do our interactions bring out the best in me and in her?
- Would she help me move forward instead of holding me back?
- Do the qualities I admire in her complement my strengths and resources?

★ There are benefits to having more than one Goal Sister (more support, different kinds of feedback) and there are drawbacks (longer meetings, more difficulty in scheduling meetings). You'll have to weigh the pros and cons in making your choice.

★ When you meet with your potential Goal Sister, share your goals and tell her about the kind of support you'd like to receive for reaching them. Ask her about her goals and assess her readiness for change. If you decide she's the one, ask if she feels the same way. If it's a go, congratulations! If not, meet with the next woman on your list until you find your Goal Sister.

Questions

★ *What gifts and talents are you willing to share with your Goal Sister?*

★ *What complementary qualities are you looking for in a Goal Sister?*

Chapter 3

Preparing the Way for Your Success

Y ou flip through the pages of your calendar, conscious of the jotted notes and numbers — and all the responsibilities they represent. It's overwhelming! It's the easiest math equation you've ever done: too many tasks and not enough hours to complete them in. "How am I going to find time for the Goal Sister process," you wonder, "when every day is full?" By the time you're through writing a report, tending to your kids and/or partner, running errands, paying bills, going to a board meeting, catching up with friends, walking the dog, calling your mom, reading your e-mail, and washing the last load of dishes, there simply isn't any time left for you. This seems to be the reality for so many of us. Yet the heart of the Goal Sister process assists you in creating the pockets of time you can't yet see in your life.

"Wow! That's worth the price of this book," you think. "Finding time for me would be great! Where do I start?" The good news is that you've already started. By seriously considering the power of support in your life and by recognizing your desire for it, you've set the stage for accomplishment and success. If you've been writing your responses to the exercises in your journal, you've already made progress in taking time for yourself.

Ann and Michelle's Story

The beginning of our time together as Goal Sisters may be like your beginning with your Goal Sister. We were both busy. We had highly responsible jobs that involved tons of paperwork. We traveled frequently for work. When we were in the office, our phones rang regularly with requests for our knowledge, time, and attention. People constantly stopped by our offices to check in or to gossip. The boss or a coworker usually needed some information before the end of the day. Outside of work, one of us volunteered at her church while the other volunteered at her children's school. It seemed like every minute was scheduled.

We realized that we couldn't give a lot of time to our new Goal Sister friendship. We liked each other and were intrigued by each other's lives, but to learn about each other in depth would require more time.

So we started small by focusing on something we could easily discuss once a week within our allotted lunch hour: career changes. We both identified the types of change we wanted to make. We listened to each other, then repeated what we heard. This feedback pointed out possible immediate goals that would move us toward our bigger goals. We began to identify tasks that we could accomplish in a day or a week. We were honest with each other about what we could and couldn't do, and we quickly became excited about being in action to have our dreams come true, no matter how small the steps seemed at the time.

Our story illustrates how the Goal Sister process starts off slowly and requires minimal in-person time. Only an hour a week! We met over lunch, but you may find it more convenient to meet over coffee before the start of your day, or maybe in the evening when someone can watch your kids. As you continue with the process, you'll probably want to spend more time with your Goal Sister. Talking about your dreams and goals can help you see which parts of your life you can let go of or minimize. We encourage you to make "carving out more time in my schedule" one of the goals you work toward with your Goal Sister.

Putting Yourself First

Imagine someone taking a photograph of your life and sending it to us. What would you be doing in the photo? Would we see you at your job, handling various responsibilities and attending meetings? Would we see you as a mom, partner, daughter, sister, friend, lover, aunt, grandmother, niece, foster mom, sister-in-law, cousin — hugging loved ones, picking up after everyone, offering kind words, staying connected? Maybe we'd see you volunteering for a meaningful cause or enjoying a favorite hobby. We might see you attending your church, temple, or other sacred place. Would we have a hard time seeing you taking care of yourself? Would that part of you be in the out-of-focus corner of the photograph? Would that part be missing from the photo altogether? For many of us, taking care of ourselves is either in the background of our lives or nonexistent.

A big part of preparing yourself to be a Goal Sister is adjusting your focus to include more self-care in the forefront of your life. By "self-care" we mean:

- Saying "no" to requests for your time;
- Giving yourself time to breathe, to just sit, to daydream;
- Exercising, moving your body, increasing your physical strength;
- Eating foods that are healthy for you and cutting back on foods that aren't; and
- Making time to create, play, and enjoy your hobbies.

You've probably heard a self-help expert talk about how increasing self-care can lead to a more balanced and fulfilling life. It all sounds so clichéd, but guess what? We're part of the self-care chorus, too. We know it works because we've put ourselves last before, and we definitely prefer being closer to the front of the line. As your Goal Sisters, we're going to encourage you to put your needs right up there with ours.

Michelle's Story

A few years into our Goal Sister friendship, Ann loaned me her copy of Cheryl Richardson's Take Time for Your Life. *I was intrigued when I flipped through the book. Cheryl was describing me: I was living a "work-centered" life. My program-evaluation consulting business was thriving, I had recently started a part-time job telecommuting to a research firm in Virginia, and my husband and I were in the throes of designing a marital toolkit. You could say that my life was focused on work! Cheryl's suggestion to adopt an "extreme self-care" approach — and her stories of clients who did so — piqued my interest. But did I read her book and follow her seven-step process? No. Instead, I launched into several years of intense focus on my career. Why? Because I could. My children were nine and seven years old, and they were plugged in to school and after-school care, which meant that I finally had more time to develop my career.*

Little did I know that I was moving from a life focused primarily on my family to a life focused primarily on my career — and that this shift would leave me feeling exhausted all the time, out of balance, and unhappy with how I looked and felt. At that point in my life, I rarely allowed time for taking care of myself. When I did, it usually centered on a family activity or a walk around the block to clear my head.

Thankfully, through the Goal Sister process, I realized that I was substituting one extreme focus for another. By talking

*with Ann about goals, I was able to see how my extreme focus
on work had placed my family farther down the priority list,
with self-care disappearing altogether.*

We realize that putting your needs first may not be your top
priority right now. That's okay. We suggest that you slowly bring
self-care into the forefront of your life, get used to seeing it as one
of your goals, and take action to make it happen when you're
ready. The Goal Sister process is, after all, not about squeezing you
into a "one size fits all" program; you and your Goal Sister will
adapt it to fit who you are, your life situation, and who you want
to become.

Identifying Your Desires

Imagine yourself at the end of your day. You've finished putting
away the dishes and you're about to turn off the lights when your
phone rings. "Who could be calling at this hour?" "It's your Fairy
Goal Mother," answers the voice on the phone. "I'm coming over
right now to ask you an important question." Before you can
respond — poof! — your Fairy Goal Mother materializes. Smiling
at you with twinkling eyes, she asks, "So, my dear, what do you
want for your life?" You want to just say, "I don't know; I haven't
given it much thought." But after thinking for a moment, you say,
"I want to have enough money for my family to be comfortable,
and I'd like a better job." Your Fairy Goal Mother smiles and says,
"That's a start, my dear. You might want to get more specific about
your desires if you're going to begin to work with your Goal Sister." You start to say something, but she looks at her watch and
interrupts: "Oh my, I really must be on my way! Make sure you
know what you want before you meet with your Goal Sister!" And
— poof! — she disappears.

Your Fairy Goal Mother is right; if you're not sure what you
want, how can you expect to get it — much less have the support

to achieve it? As a Goal Sister, you'll work diligently to question and encourage your Goal Sister and yourself to dream big, then design smaller action steps to reach those goals. But before you do that, we think it's essential for you to be clear about what you want to work on. "But where do I start?" you wonder. If you become still and listen to your inner nudgings and your gut instincts, you're likely to get a glimpse of what you want and need in your life. We encourage you to pay more attention to that inner guidance.

Exercise 3.1: Your Wish List

In their book *The Aladdin Factor,* Jack Canfield and Mark Victor Hansen provide a "101 wishes" exercise that we've found to be both fun and enlightening. We've adapted this exercise by reducing it to fifty wishes. Take out your journal now and complete fifty "I wish...." statements; you'll soon turn these into goal statements. Examples of our wishes are:

- I wish Donna's pettiness didn't bother me.
- I wish I would take better care of myself.
- I wish Dan would ease up on himself.
- I wish I could practice mindfulness daily.
- I wish we could finish decorating the house.

Don't be stingy and stop before you list fifty wishes! Imagine how astounded your Fairy Goal Mother will be next time she visits and finds out that you held yourself back! Go ahead: Brainstorm like crazy and write that list of fifty wishes now.

Transforming Your Wishes into Goals

Wouldn't it be nice if your Fairy Goal Mother visited you right now? You could show off your list of wishes and use her wand to turn them into goals. But she doesn't visit often — and, besides, you don't need her wand to transform your wishes. You have everything you need at your disposal: your ongoing commitment, your optimism, your journal, your pen or pencil, and us. Let's get to it, shall we?

Exercise 3.2: Goals Galore

Begin this exercise by writing each of the following ten goal categories at the top of ten new pages in your journal:

- Job/career
- Physical and emotional health
- Significant other
- Family and friends
- Spirituality
- Money
- Personal growth
- Environment
- Creativity and play
- Volunteer service

Turn back to your list of fifty wishes. It's time to change each wish into a goal and place it in the appropriate goal category. We suggest that you do this one wish at a time, using a three-step process:

1. Determine which goal category the wish falls under. It may fall under two or more categories, but choose the most applicable one.

2. Transform the wish into a goal. We suggest that you do this by crossing off unrelated words and adding new words to complete the action statement.

3. Write your new goal under the goal category you selected.

Here's how we transformed our wishes from Exercise 3.1 into goals and categorized them:

- Job/career: "I wish my coworker Donna's pettiness didn't bother me" becomes "Figure out how to manage my feelings around Donna's pettiness."

- Physical and emotional health: "I wish I would take better care of myself" becomes "Take better care of myself."

- Family and friends: "I wish Dan would ease up on himself" becomes "Talk with Dan about easing up on himself."

- Spirituality: "I wish I could practice mindfulness daily" becomes "Practice mindfulness daily."

- Environment: "I wish we could finish decorating the house" becomes "Finish decorating the house."

Repeat the three-step process for each of your fifty wishes. If you have trouble transforming and categorizing any of your wishes, move on to the next one. You can always return to this exercise when you meet with your Goal Sister.

Extra Nudging

After you finish Exercise 3.2, give yourself a treat. Whether you buy yourself flowers, burn your favorite scented candle, snuggle up with a good book, or take an afternoon stroll with someone you love, you deserve to celebrate the great strides you have made toward defining who you want to be. Refuel and rejuvenate before moving on to the next step in the Goal Sister process.

Selecting Your Goals

You're pumped up! You've generated fifty wishes, turned them into fifty goals, and sorted your goals into ten categories. "I wonder when I'll get to select the goals I want to work on," you muse. Then you feel a tap on your shoulder. You turn around and it's your Fairy Goal Mother. "Hello, dear, I thought I'd pop in and keep you from making a terrible mistake." You look at her incredulously. She continues: "You should really educate yourself about the ins and outs of goals before you select the ones you want to focus on. Ann and Michelle can help you with that." She kisses you on the cheek and adds, "By the way, my dear, I won't be stopping by any more. You're in good hands with your Goal Sisters." Then — poof! — she disappears. Your Fairy Goal Mother is right again. We're here for the long haul, and we're more than happy to share with you our version of "Goals 101" before you prioritize your goals.

Goals 101

There are two important issues to consider before selecting specific goals to focus on: the "size" of your goals, and your timetable for achieving them. Like soft drinks at your favorite restaurant, goals come in a variety of sizes: small, medium, and large. Each size comes with its own set of timelines: immediate, intermediate, and long-term. And each has a different set of requirements. The examples below summarize the characteristics of various goal sizes:

- **Large Goals:** "Move to a new city," "Stay tobacco-free," "Adopt a child." You can expect to achieve Large Goals in a year or more. Large Goals usually involve making a series of lifestyle changes. You will probably need to obtain a lot of information and enhance your skills along the way to achieving these goals. In goal lingo, that means accomplishing and maintaining many Small and Medium Goals before achieving your Large Goals.

- **Medium Goals:** "Call my parents weekly," "Complete the final report," "Finalize my Website design." You can expect to accomplish your Medium Goals in six months to a year, and you'll probably need to achieve and maintain several Small Goals before you reach your Medium Goal. Sometimes achieving Medium Goals requires that you obtain specific information or refine your skills. These action steps are typically designated as Small Goals.

- **Small Goals:** "Stop bringing home work files," "Cook a new healthy dish this week," "Start a gratitude journal." You can expect to achieve Small Goals immediately or within a month. Achievement of Small Goals doesn't require much information gathering or skill enhancement before you launch into action. Small Goals are often the steps you take toward achieving Medium Goals, but they can also be stand-alone goals.

Now that you have a better understanding of why the size of your goals matters, here's an example that demonstrates the relationships among the different goal sizes:

Physical and emotional health:

Large Goal:	Be healthy and fit
Medium Goals:	Lose ten pounds by the end of July
	Increase my energy level
	Exercise daily
	Increase awareness of the stress in my life that leads me to overeat
Small Goals:	Stop eating at fast-food restaurants
	Stop buying and eating cheese
	Do Tae Bo three times a week
	Eat oatmeal for breakfast five days a week
	Go to bed by 10:00 every night
	Drink eight glasses of water every day
	Keep an exercise and food journal
	Decrease weekly alcohol intake

Did you notice anything about these goals? Some goals have an expected achievement date, while others don't. You and your Goal Sister can decide how stringent you want to be about assigning expected achievement dates. We use dates when there is a specific deadline ("complete final report by end of September") or when a target date would help us achieve the goal. Otherwise, we expect to achieve Small Goals immediately or within a month, Medium Goals within six months to a year, and Large Goals within a year or more.

Did you notice that there are more Small Goals than Medium Goals, and more Medium Goals than Large Goals? Achieving Large Goals usually involves reaching several Medium Goals over an extended period of time, and even more Small Goals. Consequently, in order to achieve a Large Goal of being fit and healthy, you would need to achieve and maintain several Medium Goals after reaching many Small Goals. If you achieve several of your Medium Goals over a period of six months to a year, you will probably accomplish your Large Goal of being healthy and fit.

Exercise 3.3: Sizing Up Your Goals

Now it's time for you to rank your goals. Take out your journal and turn to your goal category pages. For each category, look over your list of goals and write an "L" next to the Large Goals that will require long-term efforts, an "M" next to the Medium Goals that will require ongoing achievement of many Small Goals, and an "S" next to the Small Goals that will require you to take immediate action without much information gathering or skill development. Do this for every goal in each goal category. You may need to do this exercise in several sittings.

On Your Mark

Now that you've passed Goals 101, let's work on selecting the goals you want to focus on. We call these your "priority goals."

Exercise 3.4: And Your Priority Goals Are...

Turn to the goal category pages in your journal. As you flip through the pages, notice which goals catch your attention. Which goals represent actions that you've wanted to take for a long time? Which goals would you prefer to shelve for now? Which Large Goals seem impossible to achieve? Which Small and Medium Goals seem doable? Which goals are you most motivated to work on? As you scan your goals, make a new list of the ones you're most interested in pursuing first.

Now scan your list of potential priority goals, looking for the three you want to work toward first. It doesn't matter if these goals are in the same goal category or different ones. We want you to limit yourself to three priority goals for now because we want you to succeed. We don't want you to be weighed down with too many goals at the start. Carefully consider your narrowed selection of priority goals and circle up to three of them.

Congratulations, Goal Sister! Choosing your first set of priority goals is a big step. While you have chosen up to three priority goals, you will probably work toward one goal at a time until you get in the habit and rhythm of achieving your goals.

One Goal at a Time?

Most self-help authors who write about goal-setting suggest that their readers first accomplish one goal at a time, then another, then another. That said, we're willing to bet that working toward one goal will affect other areas of your life, and that you'll eventually be faced with the prospect of working on multiple goals.

Michelle's Story

When Ann and I began meeting as Goal Sisters, I was a one-goal woman: I wanted to start my own program-evaluation consulting business. That goal encompassed a lot of smaller steps along the way: Learn to use QuickBooks Pro to keep track of my time, activities, invoices, and payments; familiarize myself with my new tax requirements; read books about women who leave the corporate world and start their own businesses. Ann gave me a copy of Rebecca Maddox's audiotape, Inc. Your Dreams. *When I completed Rebecca's program, I had a new confidence that I was suited to run my own business.*

Back then, it didn't occur to me that working toward one goal would affect other areas of my life. But guess what happened? Spending more and more of my free time on launching

*my consulting business began to negatively affect my attitude
at work and my relationship with my family. I might have
thrown in the towel without support from Ann and my husband; they urged me to continue making progress toward my
business goals while addressing the other areas of my life.*

Accomplishing a single goal, then noticing that other areas in
your life need improvement, is like replacing the carpet in your
living room. You stand back to admire how beautiful the colors
are, how fresh the new carpet makes the room appear — then you
notice how worn and dingy your furniture, drapes, and walls look
next to your new carpet. Don't you hate that? We don't particularly like it either. That's why we advocate listing goals in multiple
areas of your life even though you may not work toward all of
them simultaneously. By selecting priority goals, you acknowledge
that it's not feasible to work on every area of your life at once. But
by listing your goals for several areas of your life, you'll be ready to
launch into them when the time is right.

Envisioning Your Success

The next step involves imagining how you want your life to be
when you have achieved your priority goals. Like many self-help
authors and life coaches, we espouse the value of visualizing your
achievements. It might sound cheesy or over-the-top-New-Age,
but it works. Give visualization a chance; you have nothing to lose but
your cynicism.

Exercise 3.5: A Day in Your Future Life

Take out your journal and select one of your priority goals.
Close your eyes and imagine yourself reaching that goal by
the anticipated date. What are you doing and where are you

doing it? Who is with you? How do you feel, and how do others respond to you? What do you see, feel, smell, hear, and taste? Give yourself five minutes to imagine all of this. Now write down your experiences, using the present tense. Here are examples of our visualizations:

Spirituality: Practice mindfulness daily.

I see myself, eight months from now, sitting on my bed and glancing over at the small shrine I've created in the corner. The room is quiet except for the beautiful flute music playing. I smell my favorite incense burning. I am reading passages from my new mindfulness book. I practice a breathing exercise. My breathing slows down. I notice my intrusive thoughts and let them flow through me. I feel centered and ready to start my day.

Money: Manage my money better.

It's a year from now, and I am retrieving my bills from the mailbox. Instead of tossing my phone bill and my mortgage statement into a pile of junk mail, I open each bill, affix a stamp to the payment envelope, and place it on my desk. Now I am shopping online for a present for my friend; I decide to buy her something from a store in town to save money on postage. I look at my checkbook and notice that I have fifty dollars more this month to cover my expenses. I congratulate myself for being more mindful of my spending this month.

Environment: Finish decorating the house.

I'm reclining in my favorite chair, looking around our home at the beautifully painted walls and decorations. We have worked hard for nine months to finish decorating our home, and it was worth it. I'm happy that we took the time to arrange our favorite photographs in the entry hall. I walk down the hallway and peek into my children's rooms; they reflect my children's personalities, and they turned out even better than expected. Our home truly reflects who we are.

Once you've imagined how you want your life to be for each of your priority goals, you'll have little trouble identifying the gap between what you want and where you are now. Ann's story further illustrates this point.

Ann's Story

Shortly after my mom died in 1987, I was trying to decide what I wanted to do with my life. I had lots of ideas, but I didn't know what to focus on. I met a woman named Jane who did career counseling, and I made an appointment with her. Jane asked me to describe the kind of work I enjoyed, and I immediately began rattling off a number of potential employment ideas. Without pressure or expectation, Jane suggested that I focus on the idea that I became most animated about. That was the beginning of the Cancer Support Network that I founded in Bloomington, Illinois.

Jane told me about a process she'd learned from her mentor, Barbara Sher, coauthor of Wishcraft: How to Get What You Really Want. *Beginning with a goal, you work backward to identify obstacles, create a timeline to address them, and decide who can help you realize the goal. This approach worked for me; I liked the assumption that my goal would become a reality. Barbara Sher's approach supported the next part of the process, which I arrived at on my own: visualization.*

Every day, I got quiet and pictured myself achieving my goal of creating a place for people with cancer to come and receive support and information. I added details to the image that contributed to my feeling of success. I saw in my mind the path to my goal and the benefits it would offer. This helped me fill in the gap between my vision and what was happening in the now. I imagined how I would truly feel when I knew I'd met my goal. I heard the reactions of cancer survivors and their families expressing gratitude for the benefits they would experience as a result of receiving the help they needed. I ended by giving thanks in prayer for this completed vision to happen in its right timing.

I bought Wishcraft *and did the exercises one by one. I loved filling a notebook with the ideas that started to flow based on the exercise questions. I enjoyed dreaming big and asking myself, "Why not?" All the while, I was reading about others who were living their dreams, inspiring me to live my own. I also continued checking in with Jane for support and additional coaching.*

As I worked through these steps, it became clearer and clearer to me that this particular goal was mine to do at that time. I believe that if it had not been the right goal for me to work toward, I would have gone on to the next idea, using the same process. For me, the combination of goal-setting and visualization worked well.

Visualization not only helps you to imagine how you will feel when you accomplish your goals, but it often highlights the actions that you might take to achieve them. For instance, visualizing yourself achieving your "spend more time together with my boyfriend" goal may lead you to imagining yourself and your boyfriend happily eating a home-cooked dinner you prepared, planning a weekend escape together over dinner, and later cuddling on the couch while watching a scary movie.

Visualization of your goal achievement can also give you clues to unexpected actions you might take to achieve your goals. Using the above example, your visualization may surprisingly include you having a candid discussion with your boss about cutting back your evening hours. You may not have anticipated that a discussion with your boss would help you to achieve your "spend more time together with my boyfriend" goal, but it might, and it may be worth your while to add that goal onto your priority list.

Sometimes visualizing your goal achievements can give rise to your doubts and fears. Don't be discouraged if that happens, Goal

Sister. We have been there, and frankly, we see this as an opportunity for you to work through your doubts and fears as you achieve your goals. We show you how to do that in chapters 5 and 7. You'll come to believe, as we do, that anything that arises during a visualization has the potential to assist you in achieving your goals.

Preparing Your Loved Ones

Before you and your Goal Sister embark on your new friendship, we encourage you to prepare yourself and your loved ones — both emotionally and mentally — for this next phase of your life. Entering into the Goal Sister process can affect the people who are close to you. Seeing you make changes in your life may inspire them, but it may also be intimidating. For that reason, we suggest that you inform your partner, roommate, closest friends, and/or family members about your plans.

It's easy to see how making time for your success and identifying your desires and priorities will help you stay focused on achieving your goals. It's just as important that you familiarize your friends and family with the Goal Sister process so that they can support your efforts and understand their role in your success. Talk with them casually about the Goal Sister process and what it means for you. Get a sense of their opinions about your new friendship and commitment. You might think that their support is a given, but we strongly suggest that you confirm it.

Why do we emphasize this? Because when you're truly focused on your desired outcomes, your attention will be divided among your roles as a Goal Sister, family member, friend, and partner. Can you play all of these roles? Of course you can. Will your personal relationships feel the strain of your new Goal Sister friendship? Maybe. Describing the process and your degree of involvement to the people close to you is vital to thwarting misconceptions and garnering their support.

Exercise 3.6: All for One and One for All

To familiarize the people closest to you with your new Goal Sister role, we suggest that you do an activity we first discovered in Rebecca Maddox's book, *Inc. Your Dreams.* It involves setting up a special meeting with each person who supports you, including your children, for the sole purpose of talking about your plans for becoming a Goal Sister. You may want to refer to chapter 1 as you describe what a Goal Sister is and what the process involves. This discussion will help those you care about understand how they'll benefit and how they can support you. Prior to each discussion, complete the following sentences in your journal:

1. In order to pursue my goals and dreams, what I need from you is:

2. In order to pursue my goals and dreams, what I want from you is:

Why is it necessary to distinguish between your needs and your wants? We believe it's important to help those we care about recognize the level of support we require in relation to a particular goal. It's also important to encourage them to think about ways to go beyond meeting our needs, all the way to satisfying our wants. We believe that you and the people in your life, working together, can negotiate appropriate responses for all parties.

Examples of your needs and wants might include:

- For you to be comfortable with my spending some weekend mornings working toward my goals

- To be supportive of my new Goal Sister friendship

- To ask me about my new Goal Sister friendship
- To ask me how you can support me when I get stressed out
- To tell me when you're uncomfortable about the choices I'm making and why
- To trust that putting my needs first is going to be better for me and for us

Before meeting with the people in your life, also ask them to think about and write down their answers to the following questions:

1. What I need from you right now is:
2. What I want from you right now is:

Remember that you'll all be thinking about and writing your responses to these statements *prior* to your meetings. To reduce the element of surprise, we encourage you to casually discuss your new role as a Goal Sister with the people in your life prior to your meeting. This will give them an inkling about how your new commitment to the Goal Sister process might impact your current relationships, allowing them time to think about their needs.

When you meet, give yourselves plenty of time to talk through both sets of responses. This is an important exchange of information; don't just breeze through it. Focus on what the other person says. Don't take notes or ask questions; simply be present as the person talks. Ask for the same attentiveness when you talk. Generate possible solutions together so that each of your needs can be met.

The support of your loved ones adds a wonderful dimension to your work with your Goal Sister. If you take the time now to share the process with them, you'll reap big rewards down the road.

Chapter 3 Summary

★ The Goal Sister process starts out slowly and requires minimal in-person time: Only an hour a week! You might meet over coffee or for lunch. Talking about your goals can help you see which parts of your life you can let go of or minimize to make time for working toward your goals.

★ Gradually bring self-care into the forefront of your life. You might eat healthier foods, take time to sit and daydream, increase your exercise level, say "no" to requests for your time, or make time to enjoy your hobbies.

★ How do you want your life to be different? Write down your wishes and transform them into goals using the exercises in this chapter. Sort your goals into the following categories:

- Job/career
- Physical and emotional health
- Significant other
- Family and friends
- Spirituality
- Money
- Personal growth
- Environment
- Creativity and play
- Volunteer service

★ Select your priority goals based on what's most important to you now, what you're motivated to change, and how much time you have to dedicate to your goals. It's okay to have a variety of Small, Medium, and Large priority goals, but you'll probably work on one priority goal at a time. Your other priority goals will be ready for you when the time is right.

★ Visualizing yourself reaching your goals helps you imagine how your success will feel. It can also help you highlight the steps toward achieving your goals and identify the gap between what you want and where you are now.

★ As you begin to move forward, talk with your significant others about what the Goal Sister process means to you and how it might affect your relationships. Having their understanding and support will be a big help!

Questions

★ *If your Fairy Goal Mother appeared before you right now and asked you what you want for your life, how would you answer her?*

★ *How can you take better care of yourself this week?*

Part II

Living La Vida Goal Sister

Chapter 4

Connecting with Your Goal Sister

"I'm meeting with my Goal Sister today!" you exclaim to your friends, loved ones, and coworkers. "I can't wait to start our new friendship!" What more could you ask for, right? How about knowing the specifics of a typical Goal Sister meeting: what to wear, what to bring, and how to share your goals with each other? Don't panic, dear Goal Sister, we'll clue you in on all the details.

The Details

As Goal Sisters, we give a lot of thought to the details of our meetings. Deciding how we want to spend our time together and what we want to focus on helps energize the process. Thinking about where to meet and what to share with each other makes our time together fun. Counting down the days to our upcoming meeting reinforces our commitment to achieving success.

What to Wear
Come as you are from work, exercising, being out and about, or hanging out at home — dressed up or down. Spending time with

your Goal Sister isn't about looking good and showing off your fin-
ery; it's about accepting each other "as is" and focusing on your
goals and dreams.

What to Bring

After using the Goal Sister process for many years, we've learned
that it pays to be prepared. We suggest that you bring the following items to meetings:

- Cash, credit card, or other means to pay for food and
  drinks if you're going out
- Your journal or lined notebook
- Pens and markers
- Your daily planner or electronic organizer
- Self-help books that you're reading or want to share
- Your list of goals and any related notes you've written
- Anything else of interest to you and your Goal Sister

Don't forget to also bring your open mind, listening ear, and
sense of humor — and leave your judgments, sarcasm, and criticisms at the proverbial door!

Where to Meet

Get together in a place that's away from your regular routine; this
will help move your thinking and actions "out of the box." Consider places like restaurants, coffeehouses, cafés, and bookstores.
Depending on where you go, you can bring your own food and
drink from home or buy it when you get there. If you need to
meet at each other's homes or at the office, be sure to make the
necessary arrangements to limit distractions (get child care, turn
off the phone, put a "do not disturb" sign on the office door).

Ten Common Courtesies

1. Honor your meeting times. If you need to reschedule, let your Goal Sister know as soon as possible.

2. Leave your cell phone on vibrate mode (in case of an emergency) and agree to check messages at the end of the meeting.

3. Establish a "Dutch treat" rule for meals and outings. This cuts down on the discussion of whose turn it is to pay and all that goes with it.

4. Attend the meeting alone: no children, no pets; they can be distractions.

5. Leave other distractions — thoughts of errands to run, bills to pay, et cetera — outside your meeting.

6. Be present with your Goal Sister, focusing on her questions, progress, and goals.

7. Honor your Goal Sister's requests to keep information confidential.

8. Be respectful of your Goal Sister and don't interrupt her when she has the floor.

9. Be considerate in the way you come across, both verbally and nonverbally.

10. Be ready to offer your support, motivation, and interest to your Goal Sister.

Ann and Michelle's Story

When we first started meeting, we liked to get together during our lunch hour at restaurants within five to ten minutes of where we worked. We arrived at the designated place before the noon rush so that we wouldn't have to spend too much

*time looking for parking or waiting for a table. We appreci-
ated restaurants that had friendly staff, good service, fair
prices, and plenty of room for us to spread out our stuff and
stay awhile. We also liked places that were well lit and offered
healthful meals.*

*We stayed away from places that were too noisy, too cold,
or too smoky. We also avoided places where we knew our
coworkers liked to eat; not only was it distracting to bump
into them, but it could also be awkward. For example, one
time we met at our favorite deli; we were enjoying our gour-
met sandwiches and talking about how Michelle was going to
leave her job, when in walked her boss and his wife.*

"Hi, how's it going?"

"Good, you two eating lunch?"

*"Yep, and we're talking about all the things Michelle's
doing to start her own business before she quits working
for you."*

*Okay, we never actually had that conversation, but you
can imagine how much fun we had pretending we did!*

Being flexible about your meeting location can be good for
you and your Goal Sister. Your meetings don't have to revolve
around eating; you can go to a park, the lobby of a relaxing hotel,
or other quiet places that don't discourage talking, hanging out,
laughing, dreaming, problem solving, and goal achieving. A
change of scenery might be a great boost for your creativity.

When and How Long to Meet

The best time of day to meet is entirely up to you and your Goal
Sister, based on your needs and schedules. When we first started
meeting, we could both easily get together over lunch for an hour
or so. We recommend that you meet for at least an hour, and up
to two hours depending on your needs. If making plans at the last
minute works well for you and your Goal Sister, check in with

each other before you meet to see where you feel like going and how much time you have to spend together.

Exchanging Gifts

You and your Goal Sister might consider exchanging gifts. Neither of us remembers how this ritual of ours got started, but we've been doing it for quite a while. If it works for you, great; if not, that's okay, too.

We usually start each Goal Sister meeting with our gift exchange. Gifts we've given in the past include stickers, markers, candles, and copies of our favorite CDs. These gifts don't need to be extravagant; they just let your Goal Sister know you've been thinking about her and found something that reminds you of her and her dreams. You might include an inspiring card to go along with your gift. However you do it, don't let exchanging gifts become an obligation, competition, or one more thing you have to add to your "To Do" list. Exchanging gifts is meant to be a fun addition to your meetings and your Goal Sister friendship.

Michelle's Story

I'm always touched by my Goal Sister gifts from Ann. She puts together a pretty gift bag, lined with different-colored tissues and filled with individually wrapped items. She always includes a card that she's carefully picked to express her gratitude for our friendship or her expectations of a productive, fun meeting. What makes Ann's gifts special is the thought, creativity, and care she puts into them. Knowing that I admire Mary Engelbreit's work, Ann has given me socks, note cards, and dishtowels sprinkled with Mary's cherry designs. After I decided to move back to Hawaii, she gave me hula-girl swizzle sticks, aloha-shirt sticky notes, and palm-tree glasses. When I hit a creative block, Ann gave me audiotapes and books to help me find my muse, blank journals, and a kid's paintbrush

*set. At each meeting, Ann also brings several relevant maga-
zine articles she's clipped for me. Yep, I'm blessed with a gen-
erous, big-hearted Goal Sister!*

*My gifts for Ann, on the other hand, are usually un-
wrapped; they're in the bags I bought them in or a gift bag
she's previously given me. As much as I'd like to say that I
always include a carefully selected card for my Goal Sister,
I don't; especially when my kids were younger, I simply didn't
have time for those extra touches. Before our meetings, I'm
usually stressing out about all the things I have to get done so
that I can focus on Goal Sisters when I'm with Ann. That's a
bit of a cop-out, I know. I'm grateful that Ann recognizes the
other side of my excuse: that my true gift to her is my rapt
attention during our time together.*

There's another gift that we Goal Sisters give each other through
our interactions. It's not a gift that you can hold in your hands,
nor is it a gift that has a particular monetary value. It is the gift of
friendship and support.

Ann's Story

*I loved my job at the substance-abuse treatment agency in
Bloomington, Illinois. I loved it for most of the five years I
worked there. But if you'd talked to me during those last few
months of employment, you would have talked to a burned-
out, discouraged, tired counselor. What changed? My office
was still mine. My great coworkers were still on the team. My
clients continued to teach me great lessons. My supervisors
were still understanding and supportive of my work. The paycheck still registered the same fair amount, and I'd even
recently received a bonus. What changed?*

*It was me. I had simply shifted my focus to the next phase
of my life. In conversations with friends, it was hard to find
anyone who understood that nothing particularly bad had*

happened at work to upset me or to show me that I needed to move on. Indeed, most friends expressed concern that I could so easily leave such a great situation; they wondered if I had really thought about what I'd be giving up.

Enter Michelle Pillen. Like a breath of fresh air, Michelle asked me, "What's your target date for moving on?" With that one question, she let me know that she believed I was doing what was right for me. She had confidence in my ability to discern my highest good, and she was saying, "Go for it." Wow. I kicked into action at an even higher pace, knowing that my Goal Sister saw the same vision for me.

I believe that this is a key to knowing who your Goal Sister should be: She offers support for your goals and vision. She doesn't impose her thoughts on you, nor does she accept bribes from your family and friends to convince you that their way is really your way! This is a huge gift between friends; don't underestimate its value, and always give thanks for it.

Sharing Your Stuff

In addition to sharing our list of priority goals, we make time during each meeting to show each other our "stuff." Some of the "stuff" we share relates directly to achieving our goals. We might share stuff we want to brag about (copies of magazine articles we've written, letters of interest in our artwork), stuff we're working on (self-help books we're reading, journals we're keeping), stuff we've completed (final reports, business plans, training curricula), and stuff we've purchased (water bottles, financial software, calendar pages). The other "stuff" we share relates to what we believe might be of interest to our Goal Sister. Examples include magazine articles, books, audiotapes, and other resources we've been collecting since our last get-together. The idea is to inspire each other with resources and milestones that keep us moving forward.

Orienting Each Other to Your Goals

Your first few meetings with your Goal Sister will probably be focused on getting to know each other and exploring your dreams and goals. For the early discussions, we suggest that you ask each other what it's been like generating your wish list, turning your wishes into goals, and selecting priority goals. For the later discussions, it's important to share your list of priority goals with your Goal Sister and ask her why she chose one priority goal over another. Knowing the motivation behind her goal selection will give you a better idea of her investment and interest in achieving that goal. Like you, your Goal Sister will probably have a variety of reasons for choosing to work on certain goals over others, including experiencing a wake-up call, being fed up with a situation, and undergoing a life transition.

Getting a Wake-Up Call

Your Goal Sister's reason for choosing her priority goals may be tied to a dramatic event that left her feeling vulnerable. We call these events "wake-up calls." For example, a woman might be interested in finding a new job because she was unexpectedly laid off as a result of downsizing. Another woman might want to quit smoking because a close friend had a heart attack. Sometimes wake-up calls result from completing an exercise recommended by a self-help author, leading to new insights and a motivation to live differently.

Being Fed Up

Some women are motivated to change because they are fed up with a situation or a relationship. For example, your Goal Sister may be sick of not being happy, sick of complaining about not being happy, and sick of being sick. Her goal might be to get herself and her life to a better place. This is actually a common motivation for many women; they want to get unstuck from the same old scenes with the same old characters doing the same old things.

Michelle's Story

My friend Josefina worked in the retail business for fifteen years. Over the years, she sold jewelry, furniture, and women's clothing at the same large department store. She started out stocking shelves and worked her way up to being a regional manager. At the peak of her retail career, Josefina quit and went back to school. When I asked her why she quit, Josefina told me that she became fed up with the parts of her job that drained her. She had a great salary, but she worked long hours. She had a staff of forty employees, but many were unreliable and irresponsible. Josefina was tired of working on holidays instead of spending them with her family. She was tired of being exhausted at the end of the workday and not having the energy to meet with friends or read science fiction, her favorite pastime. Josefina was tired of being tired.

Fortunately, Josefina chose a new career direction as a dental hygienist, which afforded her many job opportunities when she finished school. She now works regular hours, makes a good salary, and spends most holidays with her family. Whenever we reminisce about her life in the retail world, she groans. Then she laughs, shakes her head, and reminds me that it took her three years to figure out that being in the retail business wasn't a good fit for her — and twelve more years before she got fed up and left.

Being stuck in a personal or professional rut happens to the best of us. If you and your Goal Sister find yourselves in this situation, you can help each other identify these ruts, brainstorm ways to get out of them, and encourage each other as you take action. But for now, sharing what it feels like to be in these ruts and how they fuel your determination to reach your goals is the primary focus.

Going through a Transition

Not every woman's goals result from wake-up calls or from being fed up. Your Goal Sister may have the opportunity to change her life or pursue her dreams because she now has more time, more freedom, and fewer responsibilities. Such an opening can occur for a number of reasons, including having a break in a school or work schedule, children leaving home, or retirement from the workforce. The upshot is that these transitions afford her the opportunity to explore who she wants to become and try her hand at realizing her dreams. Several women in the original Goal Sister group were in this category.

Goal Sister Group Story

The Goal Sister group members were all experiencing life transitions when they started meeting on March 7, 2002. Nelda's son was about to graduate from college and move out on his own. Deborah's son and Joy's three children were all grown and living away from home. Cindy's daughter was about to leave home, and she needed less of her mother's attention. Joy and Cindy were contemplating job changes. MJ was ending her marriage and considered applying to graduate school. Even Ann and Michelle were in the midst of life transitions: Ann had recently ended the long-term relationship that had brought her to Missouri, and Michelle was preparing for her family's move from Illinois to Hawaii.

Getting Extra Help from Your Goal Sister

Once you and your Goal Sister have oriented each other to your priority goals and the motivations behind their selection, you may want to ask each other for additional brainstorming and for feedback about your timelines.

Further Brainstorming Needed

Your Goal Sister can help you generate a complete list of Small Goals that will lead to achieving your Medium and Large Goals. For example, if you have a Medium-sized priority goal in your "Friends and family" category that says, "Have more upbeat communications with Victoria," and the Small Goals in that category are linked to a different Medium Goal (e.g., "Call Aunt Sadie every week"), you will need to generate additional Small Goals. Examples of Small Goals that you and your Goal Sister might come up with are:

- Initiate phone contact with Victoria only when I'm in a good mood
- Let Victoria know when it's not a good time to talk
- Journal about why Victoria's personality pushes my emotional buttons

Remember: The more Small Goals you achieve over a period of time, the greater the likelihood that you will achieve your Medium Goals. Similarly, the more Medium Goals you achieve over a period of time, the greater the likelihood that you will achieve your Large Goals.

Ann's Story

When MaryLu and I decided to work together on our business marketing goals, we agreed by noon the next day that we both wanted more income and more clients. We set our Large Goals: five new paying clients for me, and three new paying business accounts for MaryLu. We then launched into creating the steps that would get us there. For our Medium Goals, we committed to contacting ten people a week about our services and calling five potential contacts per day. My initial

Small Goal was to call groups each day to get the contact name of whom to approach for speaking engagements, while MaryLu's Small Goal was to generate referrals for her graphic design services.

Once we had a vision of our overall plans, we went into action. My other Small Goals popped up easily: write my phone pitch, set up a database of prospects, read the newspaper daily for news of potential prospects, and so on. It was fun to receive an e-mail from MaryLu telling me that a contact had called her back and that she was scheduled to show her portfolio to a prospective client the next week. I enjoyed sharing my own news about contacting someone who seemed to truly understand life coaching and who wanted to secure my services. MaryLu and I kept track of our progress, noted our defeats, and shared our feelings about the process. We even held a "virtual party," complete with champagne and strawberries, when our first clients came on board!

MaryLu and I quickly realized that accomplishing the Small Goals was an important part of our overall success. We shifted our expectations of having new clients appearing now to celebrating the completion of each step along the way. Being aware of success at each step actually made the accomplishment of the Large Goal even sweeter. We learned that creating the plan and working it faithfully led to getting terrific results that paid off, not only now but also in the future.

Timing Is Everything

You may ask your Goal Sister for feedback on the timelines you've assigned to your priority goals. For example, if your Large-sized priority goal is "Be Board President of the Community Recycling Center," and your expected date of achievement is in less than a year, your Goal Sister may ask you questions you hadn't considered, such as:

- Have you thought about how you're going to make time in your already full schedule for this added responsibility?

- Have you asked the current board president about the average number of hours you would be expected to spend at the Community Recycling Center?

- Have you worked out an agreement with anyone to watch your children on the nights when you're attending meetings?

Based on your answers and your discussion with your Goal Sister, you might or might not decide to change your timeline.

Extra Nudging

If you had problems completing any of the exercises in chapter 3, you might want to ask your Goal Sister to help you with them. She can assist you in transforming your wishes into goals, ranking your goals, and working on any other steps you need help with. She may ask for your assistance in return. Remember: helping your Goal Sister helps you!

Just Checking In

After meeting several times and spending some time working toward your goals, you and your Goal Sister will probably want to establish a way of discussing your progress. For us, talking in an unstructured way has been successful. We take turns talking about the areas we're working on and giving brief updates on our progress. After years of meeting, a typical interaction about our goals usually goes like this:

MICHELLE: So, what's happening with your health goals? I think one of them was to "continue walking every day." How's that going?

ANN: Great! I usually go for a morning walk around my neighborhood, and sometimes I take a break from working and walk in the afternoon.

MICHELLE: How long do you typically walk for?

ANN: About twenty minutes, sometimes thirty.

MICHELLE: Wonderful! And are you feeling better physically?

ANN: I sure am. As a matter of fact, I scheduled a doctor's appointment for next week, and I'm going to ask him if I can stop taking blood-pressure pills.

MICHELLE: Cool. I'm glad you're taking better care of yourself. What about "release fast food"? How's that health goal coming?

ANN: Mostly good. I've really cut down, although I ate fast food last week on my way back from Kansas City. I just need to pack carrots and fruit when I travel so that I'm not tempted to eat bad food on the road.

MICHELLE: Sounds like a plan!

ANN: What's really been interesting about my fast-food goal is that, in general, I'm paying more attention to what I'm eating. So my overall eating has gotten healthier.

MICHELLE: That's awesome!

ANN: And how about your health goals? Are you "cutting out desserts"?

MICHELLE: Yep, I'm doing better at that — especially when we eat out. I'm not doing quite as well at home, though. Sometimes I take bites out of Bart's desserts when I need to make my sweet tooth happy.

ANN: Hmmm... So what do you do when you're tempted and you don't give in?

MICHELLE: I drink water or have a piece of fruit. Sometimes I go to bed hungry and try to distract myself.

ANN: Are those realistic ways to handle your late-night hunger?

MICHELLE: Yeah, so far. Maybe I should make a point of eating something an hour before I go to bed. That way I'll give my stomach more time for digestion, and I won't feel so guilty.

ANN: That seems reasonable. Do you still fill out your daily exercise journal?

MICHELLE: Yep, I feel very good about having maintained that new habit. It takes time to write down what I eat, how long I exercise, blah, blah, blah, but writing it down helps me pay better attention to my physical health and how it's connected to other areas of my life.

ANN: I think it's great that you've achieved that goal. Maybe I'll start my own exercise journal.

Your early interactions with your Goal Sister may differ from our established interactions. For instance, you'll probably only talk about one goal category at a time, and no more than one to two priority goals in that category. You and your Goal Sister might also ask each other more questions than we do about the steps you're taking to achieve your goals. That's a great way to get to know each other's strengths and struggles. Another way in which your interactions may differ from ours is that you and your Goal Sister may talk more about the "size" of your priority goals. We're familiar with the size of each other's goals and we don't feel the need to use those labels during our progress check-ins. You and your Goal Sister, however, will probably benefit from having a better understanding of the relationships among your priority goals if you mention whether they are Small, Medium, or Large.

As you can see, our progress check-ins are usually informal. If you and your Goal Sister prefer having more structured meetings, we suggest that you negotiate how much time each person will have to share her progress, then stick to that agreement. Regardless of how you talk about your goals, remember to ask each other how you're doing with carving out time for self-care.

Discussing and Solving Problems

We always dedicate a portion of our meetings to discussing problems we're encountering in meeting our goals. Sometimes this takes a long time; other times it only takes a few minutes. We go with the flow. If one of us is stuck, we spend time brainstorming ideas and actions. Then, at our next meeting, we check in about the results of using any of the ideas we brainstormed.

After meeting for a few weeks, the Goal Sister group members got into their own rhythm of goal setting and checking in on each other's progress. They also started problem solving and giving each other feedback.

Goal Sister Group Story

As the group members paid attention to their lives, the goals they wanted to set became clear. Deborah wanted to sing more, clear out clutter, and call friends for fun. Cindy decided to read more books, see more movies, and take weekend trips with friends. Joy felt a need to play more relaxing music and do some home remodeling. And almost all of us wanted to shed a few pounds and increase our exercise regimen. A theme of self-care became established.

Once their initial goals were defined, the group members created timelines for achieving their goals, identified people who could support them, and decided how they wanted to be held accountable. Most of them responded well to target deadlines. It was helpful for Nelda to say, "I will purchase my new sewing machine by July 8, 2002," rather than "I will purchase my new sewing machine sometime in the next year." Karen felt the same way as she pinpointed a departure date from her job to open her own business. MJ felt it necessary to look far ahead as she began to balance a life based in both Hawaii and Missouri; she wanted to have a business on the mainland within a certain time period, and that would affect which months she could spend in Hawaii.

At each meeting, the group members checked in on each other's progress. They found it helpful to get suggestions about what to do if they were stuck. It was exciting to be among women who heard each other's wishes and took a sincere interest in helping one another turn them into reality. They began to really commit to the Goal Sister process.

Making a Commitment to Your Goals

After talking with your Goal Sister about your goals and the progress you've made, it's time to make a commitment about which goals you want to accomplish before your next meeting or within the next ninety days. This might mean keeping your current priority goals, revising your goal statements, changing the priority of your goals, or creating new goals.

Before you leave the meeting, we suggest that you and your Goal Sister commit to your goals verbally. Tell each other why each goal is important to you and how it will improve your life. Hearing yourself explain the importance of each goal reinforces it in your mind and heart. At the same time, you might realize that you could do more, or perhaps that you've bitten off more than you can realistically chew. If so, you can redefine and recommit before you leave the meeting.

Being Supportive through Creativity

We like to support each other's commitment to working on goals by drawing in each other's calendars or day planners. It's a fun way to help a Goal Sister remember her goals.

Ann's Story

Early in our Goal Sister friendship, when Michelle and I met at a local deli to discuss our goals, I noticed that she always had a pen in her hand. As she talked, she usually doodled; that simple act seemed to help her clarify and express whatever she was thinking. She often doodled on her calendar, which we each had out in order to commit to timelines for our various goals. I loved her drawings!

After a while, whenever I set a goal I'd ask Michelle, "Would you draw something on my calendar to remind me how much I want this?" Often the drawings weren't related to a specific goal. In fact, the first simple drawing was on July 4, 1998; she drew two firecrackers and wrote, "Bang, bang, you're free! To be who you are and want to be!" There were squiggles and dots and lots of color. There was a snake saying "Dreams do come true," and some flying hamburgers and French fries to remind me of my goal to stop eating fast food. All very effective!

Through the years, my calendar pages have evolved. Michelle now creates full-month themed pages, like the "A Day in the Life of Ann Leach" page that shows me as a mermaid writing magazine articles, coaching dolphins, and finding new clients in underwater treasure chests. Then there's a surfer riding the waves of success as an octopus reminds me not to get sucked into negative thinking.

These pages aren't just chronicles of my important calendar dates; they're works of art! You can see an example of Michelle's calendar illustrations in the inside cover of this book; imagine her playful style and motivating words appearing on my calendar every day! It's a delight and a personal reminder that my Goal Sister is with me in spirit, even if she can't be with me in person.

I've tried to reciprocate by drawing in Michelle's calendar, by the way, but I'm not the artist that she is. I've resorted to buying stickers from scrapbook stores and copying lettering. I've cut out words and images from magazines and glued them onto her calendar pages, hoping to achieve a similar look. It's a real testament to our friendship that Michelle has allowed me such freedom with her own planner!

Whether you draw in each other's calendars or put together a page of words and images to inspire each other between meetings, using creativity to support your Goal Sister in meeting her goals will liven things up and show you the value of play.

Celebrating Your Successes and Your Failures

What? Did you just read that correctly? Yes, we believe in celebrating both our successes and our failures because both experiences offer growth opportunities. We don't actually encourage Goal Sisters to pat each other on the back when you fail to meet your goals. But we do celebrate each other's willingness to see our failures as important lessons and to learn from them. That may sound schmaltzy, but it's another form of support: helping each other find the treasure among the ruins. When you find it and don't get mired down in the "I blew it" part, that's worth a song and a dance and high-fives all around!

Ann's Story

There's one thing I've learned to accept about myself: When I do something, I want to do it in a big way. I get so passionate about the purpose and the possibilities that I want the world to experience the event/cause/situation as powerfully as I do. My drive comes from a desire to share.

In the early days of HIV and AIDS education, I coordinated my agency's commemoration of World AIDS Day. I involved every department at work, including the maintenance and administrative staffs, and I worked as a liaison with community groups to gain media attention for the day. For three months, I facilitated agency-wide planning meetings, wrote press releases, made hundreds of red-ribbon pins, designed flyers, and handled the innumerable details necessary to launch such awareness-building efforts.

At one of our Goal Sister meetings, Michelle asked for an update on the event's progress. "It's going okay, but I still haven't heard from the Health Department about how they're going to help us," I replied. "It really has me bummed because, of all the departments, they should be on board with us." Then I let loose, ranting and raving about everything that wasn't happening and how slow people were about getting back to me and how I have to explain one hundred times a day why we're doing this and respond to prejudice about the topic and on and on and on. Michelle just stared at me as I pontificated about the injustice of it all.

She took a deep breath, then asked, "Ann, do you see the good you're doing? Or are you going to just stay focused on what isn't happening right now?" It was my turn to stare at her. She certainly got my attention! "You have covered all your bases. You are teaching the community about a deadly disease in every way possible, from art exhibits to news stories to discussion groups to making quilt panels to a memorial in the chapel. You have brought together groups of people who never even knew each other existed before, much less thought of working together on a project. I think you need to stop and recognize that this event is already a success."

Isn't that true? We get so caught up in the activity and the planning and the hoping and the details that we don't remember to breathe and enjoy the process. I am grateful for Michelle's pointed question and her ability to show me a different way to look at the situation. We now easily do that for each other, and it is a great blessing to our friendship.

Exercise 4.1: Lessons Learned

Here's your chance to explore the connection between your successes and your failures. Take out your journal, give some thought to the following questions, and write down your responses.

1. What have been your three greatest successes over the past three months (lost ten pounds, got a raise, learned how to network your home computers, et cetera)?

2. What lessons did you learn from each of these successes?

3. How were these lessons connected? For example, were they the same lesson you learned over and over again? Did these lessons build on each other?

4. Identify two feelings you had with each of your successes.

5. What were three of your greatest failures over the past three months (made a bad decision, missed out on a job opportunity, overspent on last month's budget, et cetera)?

6. What lessons did you learn from each of these failures?

7. How did you feel about each failure?

8. Is there some way that each failure may have been a gift in disguise? If so, identify the gift or benefit you received.

9. Were the lessons you learned from these failures connected to each other or to the successes you had during the same period?

10. What would you like to change about your definition and experience of "success"? What steps in your thinking and actions can you take in the next week to activate these changes?

11. What would you like to change about your definition and experience of "failure"? What steps in your thinking and actions can you take in the next week to activate these changes?

Using the Goal Sister process, we're asking you to reframe your definitions of success and failure. It's time for you and your Goal Sister to ease up, think "outside the box," and open your minds and hearts to greater possibilities for yourselves.

Scheduling Your Next Meeting

Before you end your Goal Sister meeting, you should schedule the next one. Take out your calendars or electronic organizers and find a mutually workable date and time. No need to decide where you'll meet right now; the important thing is to agree on a date and time. You can also schedule check-in calls between meetings to support each other until you're together again. And don't forget: e-mail works, too!

No matter how you and your Goal Sister handle the details of meeting and sharing, you will leave your meetings feeling energized, focused, and grateful for all you are creating in your life.

Chapter 4 Summary

★ There are some common courtesies to abide by when meeting with your Goal Sister:

- Let each other know as soon as possible if you need to reschedule your meeting.
- Pay for your own meals and drinks.
- Attend your meetings alone.
- Honor confidentiality.

★ When you attend Goal Sister meetings, come as you are from work, exercising, being out and about, or hanging out at home. Hold meetings in conveniently located places that are away from your regular routine.

★ Things to bring to your meetings:

- Your journal and pen
- materials to share

- Your list of priority goals
- Perhaps a small gift that reminds you of your Goal Sister

★ Design the format of your meetings to reflect the personalities and needs of you and your Goal Sister.

★ Discuss whether the motivation behind your goal selection stems from having had a wake-up call, being fed up with a situation or relationship, or being in a transition period.

★ Update each other on your progress toward achieving your goals and carving out time for yourself. Be sure to brainstorm solutions to stumbling blocks. Discuss your anticipated timelines for goal achievement.

★ Before leaving each meeting, commit to your next set of goals. Share deadlines with your Goal Sister so that she can then hold you gently accountable for reaching them successfully!

Questions

★ *In what favorite place would you like to hold your Goal Sister meetings?*

★ *What information about your life or goals would you like to share with your Goal Sister?*

Chapter 5

Cozying Up to Your Doubts and Fears

After a fun, productive meeting with your Goal Sister, you leave feeling charged up and inspired. Now what? You might begin working toward your goals as soon as you get back home or to the office, eager to get your life moving in the right direction. You might wait a day or two — even a week — before you review your goals, unsure of yourself and where to begin. You might put off doing anything about your goals until it's almost time to meet again, feeling pressure and high expectations to do more than you're ready to do yet. The truth of the matter is that facing your goals on your own is often an invitation for your doubts and fears to appear. How do we know? Because we go way back with our own doubts and fears. In this chapter, we will show you how your doubts and fears might come knocking on your door, and we'll suggest ways for you to welcome them, get close to them, use them to your benefit, and release them.

Putting Your Needs First May Cause Excuses

Sometimes our doubts and fears show up cloaked as excuses. One sure way to bring up excuses is to focus your energy on your own needs and desires. Merely thinking about putting your needs first may cause a rush of excuses to tumble out of your head:

- "There are a million things to be done; my needs will have to wait."
- "I'm the only one who knows how to do it, so I can't afford to give myself a break right now."
- "I'm doing okay, but other people really need my attention right now."

Sound familiar? Like us, you may have used these excuses before. Our favorite excuses were with us for years before we decided to release our timeworn friends. Yes, you read that right; those excuses were our friends. They protected us from having to face up to our doubts and fears. No wonder we played them over and over in our heads and said them out loud to anyone who asked why we didn't take better care of ourselves. Some self-help experts refer to excuses as broken records. Not us! We may have overplayed our excuses, but they have excellent clarity because we practiced using them a lot. We knew all their words by heart, and we could sing them to you at the slightest suggestion of putting our needs first.

Exercise 5.1: Make No Excuses

We'd like you to take out your journal. On the left side of the page, list all your excuses for why self-care isn't going to work for you. That's right; you might as well get them out now. When you're through listing your excuses on the left side, reframe your excuses into wishes on the right side of the page. For example:

Excuses	Wishes
I feel uncomfortable putting my needs first.	I would like to feel comfortable putting my needs first.
I don't have a clue where to start.	I would like to use the Goal Sister process to find out where I can start.

Ann's Story

When I think back to 1988 — the year after my mother died — I still get overwhelmed thinking about all that I did. I closed out her bank accounts, closed up her apartment, held an estate sale, sold her car, paid her remaining bills, made what seemed like hundreds of copies of the death certificate, and dealt with the accountant, the insurance company, and the Social Security office — all while answering family friends' inquiries of "Now what will you do?" and supposedly doing my own grieving. It was an amazing load to handle.

At the same time, I closed my own apartment in Kansas City, Missouri, smuggled my two cats into my mother's "no pets allowed" apartment until I found my own place, purchased a new car, took a trip to visit old family friends, and decided to move forward with plans for the cancer support organization I founded after my mom died. All of this happened in the span of five months. They were all good activities and tasks that needed to be completed, but something was missing.

The upshot of continually being in high gear was that I didn't allow my grief to come out. Taking care of the business — or busyness — of mom's death became my excuse for not allowing the grief process to happen naturally. Of course, I had my moments of missing my mom and wishing she was around for significant events, and I even told myself that I was getting through this grieving process pretty darned well. But it wasn't until exactly one year after her death that it hit me; I became physically ill with pneumonia, a sinus infection, and a sore throat. I learned that if we don't allow our emotions to express themselves directly, they'll find other ways to come out.

How I wish I'd had a Goal Sister back then! I really needed someone to gently walk with me and remind me to slow down, breathe, and allow myself to feel whatever I needed to feel.

Exercise 5.2: Becoming Aware

Over the next week, we'd like you to pay attention to how many times you put other people's needs ahead of your own. As women, we're encouraged — and sometimes expected — to put our needs last and help others first. Notice when this happens and how it feels for you. Don't forget to write about these experiences in your journal.

Michelle's Story

Back in 1997, when Zoë was seven and Kanoa was five, I started volunteering at their elementary school. I began by chaperoning field trips and baking cookies for class parties. Because I had my own consulting business and worked from home, it was easy to zoom over to the school in the middle of the day to volunteer for thirty minutes here and an hour there. I was happy to help out where I was needed.

Then I began attending monthly Parent Teacher Organization (PTO) meetings. What I heard at these meetings energized and inspired me; there were so many ways to be a part of this school's community! My efforts could make a difference, and my skills could be put to good use. That's when I unleashed the rabid volunteer in me, and she quickly took on a life of her own. I cochaired a new multicultural education committee. With another parent and several teachers, I taught second- and fourth-graders about multicultural and diversity issues. I tutored first-grade children in reading. I was a room parent. I cochaired the school's first Fall Festival.

I wanted to reduce the speed and force of my involvement, but the requests just kept coming, and it was too hard to say "no" after saying "yes" for years. So I said "yes" to participating on a districtwide committee charged with selecting science textbooks. I said "yes" to compiling and writing the results of a districtwide satisfaction survey. I said "yes" to sorting and boxing groceries for the school's monthly fundraiser. I said "yes" to cochairing that fundraising committee for a year. I said "yes" to writing a grant proposal on the school's behalf. I said "yes" to coordinating a schoolwide satisfaction survey of students, parents, and teachers. I said "yes" to chairing the games committee for the school's carnival. I just kept on saying "yes." By the time Zoë entered sixth grade, I was a burned-out volunteer. I had given a lot of myself over the previous four years, and I might have continued volunteering except that my enthusiasm was gone. Many of the parents I had enjoyed collaborating with had moved away or begun to volunteer at the junior high. A small but growing number of parent volunteers seemed more interested in backbiting, pettiness, and gossip than in making a difference and having fun.

When Kanoa started fourth grade, I saw an opportunity to end my tenure as a parent volunteer. I declined to chair or participate on any PTO committees, and I stopped attending other meetings. My only volunteer experience that year was as a room parent for Kanoa's class.

I didn't fully understand what drove my decision to stop,

but something inside me knew that my time as a parent volunteer had expired. I needed to step aside to let a fresh group of excited, interested parents take my place. I had to do it for my sake, for my family's sake, and for my business' sake. I needed to do it because I had truly lost myself in my desire to be a good volunteer. And the only way I was going to find myself was to let these duties go and give myself the time and space to figure out my next steps.

Extra Nudging

Self-care doesn't have to carry a negative connotation. Easier said than believed, right? We hope you'll make room in your beliefs to see that self-care has a valuable place in your life. Consider the following:

- Being "selfish" can also mean taking care of yourself emotionally, physically, mentally, and spiritually so that you can be a better mom, partner, friend, employee, sister, aunt, and so on.

- Self-care may mean shifting some responsibilities with grace as you make room in your life to achieve your own goals.

- Making self-care a priority may improve your relationship with yourself — especially the part of you that walks through life like a robot and the part of you that doesn't know what you want because you haven't given yourself the luxury of ever finding out.

Excuses and Failures and Fears — Oh My!

Putting your needs first isn't the only invitation for your excuses to show up; they might make an appearance when you start defining smaller steps toward achieving your goals. For example, if your Medium Goal is to manage your money better, you might have trouble generating Small Goals that will lead to your Medium Goal. Instead, you might jump right into making excuses: "It's no use trying to pay off my credit cards because I don't make enough money to make ends meet," "I don't see the point in creating a budget when I haven't ever been successful at keeping one," or "Why should I waste time trying to save money every week if I'll end up spending it on something frivolous anyway?" For some of us, the more failures we've experienced with elusive goals in the past, the less effort we want to put into new attempts at achieving these goals, and the more quickly we give up on ourselves. All of this emotional muck gives rise to limiting beliefs that may affect your approach to goal achievement.

Ann's Story

My best friend, Ted, has a belief that he calls the Blue Shirt Theory. With a few failed relationships behind him, he's hesitant to trust that process again, no matter how much his heart desires companionship and sharing. "It's like wearing a blue shirt," he explained to me. "If every time you put on a blue shirt you break out in a rash, you start to think, 'Hmmm, I guess I shouldn't wear a blue shirt anymore.'" Ted's attachment to his past failures had prevented him from working toward having a healthy relationship.

Whenever I hear this limiting belief from Ted — or when I hear similar stories from others close to me — I've learned to stop and ask myself two questions: "In what areas of my life am I holding on to old thoughts that limit and no longer serve me?" and "Are those worn-out thoughts and the fear they create keeping me from having what I say I want?"

For a long time, the answer to those questions was "yes" when it came to my role as a leader on work teams. As a team leader, I was responsible for coordinating projects and outlining the steps needed to assure our team's success. That part came easily. Then it would be time for the meeting and the presentation of my outline. The team members would inevitably stare blankly at me and at the agenda, not really engaged in the project or its outcome. Some of the thoughts that swirled through my mind after each session were "Where did I go wrong?" "Why didn't they get excited or participate in discussions?" "Maybe I didn't present the material clearly." "Maybe I didn't leave enough time for discussion." Somehow, though, we managed to muddle through the sessions together and — usually with the pressure of a deadline looming — pull it off successfully. But then there was always the next time. I got through these meetings with dread and a sense of failure. I believed that we as a team, and especially I as the team leader, could do better.

I attached myself so securely to my perceived failures that I eventually became intent on quitting, convinced that I did not have what it took to lead the team effectively. Finally, I told my supervisor that I didn't want to be a team leader anymore. I explained that I was more comfortable just being on the team and that she could count on me to do my part with 110-percent commitment. "Too bad," she said. "I need you to lead because you are the one who can see the big picture for us." I resisted. I even called in sick on the day of a planning session; I had worked myself up about it so much that I'd convinced myself I was "sick" of it, and I was completely unmotivated to strive toward improvement.

Yet when I got back to the office, there was a note from my supervisor with an idea to use for the next team meeting. Ugh!

When I realized that I was not going to get out of this role, and that the opportunities to learn and change continued to be placed in front of me, I began to let go of my sense of failure and explore how I could approach the problem differently. I shifted my thinking from having to tell the team what we needed to do to helping them identify the requirements for each other. I asked for help from other team leaders who had more success in doing these types of projects. I introduced an element of fun into the process. I accepted the fact that I was the one who needed to take the lead. Slowly, things progressed and the tasks became a bit easier. I relaxed. Having detached myself from my past failures, I rediscovered my trust in the process, and ultimately we all succeeded.

Like many of us, you may have your own experiences of past failures to rise above. We believe that it's necessary to work through whatever your blocks are in order to have the change and the success you truly want. We believe this so strongly that we've included a whole section about naming and releasing our limiting beliefs in chapter 7.

Exercise 5.3: Your Blue Shirt

Examine the closet of your mind and heart. What "blue shirts," or unresolved past failures, are hanging in your closet? Give yourself time to really go through that closet, checking behind the door and up on the top shelf. We suspect that you don't have to look too long — that your "blue shirts" are hanging right in front of you. Take out your journal and write down the ones that come to mind. Give yourself fifteen minutes to write about all these experiences or any thoughts you have about them. Then look at one of those experiences and ask yourself, "How can I make this shirt wearable again? What steps can I take to turn this failure into a success and get closer to accomplishing my goal?" Answer these questions for each one, then congratulate yourself for moving forward in overcoming your past sense of failure. Now go to your day planner and set a timetable for honoring the action steps you created.

Aligning Your Desires and Intentions with Your Actions

Which would you rather do: tell others what they want to hear about the progress you're making, or demonstrate your intentions through actions that let others know, beyond a shadow of a doubt, that you're sincere about reaching your goals? This is an easy question to answer, but often a tough one to live out. That said, we know it's easier to tell your boss, partner, or mother whatever you think they want to hear. It's easier to reassure yourself that you're being a good employee, partner, or daughter by letting others think you're doing, being, and saying what they want you to do, be, and say. It's much harder to align your words with your actions. Why? Because many times that means facing your fears head on: fear of failure, fear of success, fear of rejection.

Ann's Story

This is a good example of how one brave woman took the necessary steps to align her actions with her intentions and desires, and thus live a life true to herself. Mary Ann, a former coworker of mine, was married to a recovering alcoholic. He had not had a drink in many years, but he still exhibited the traits of an alcoholic, verbally abusing his wife and their two young children. He had strong bouts of anger, and he took his anger out on them. He constantly belittled their efforts around the house. My friend was taking positive steps to cope with the situation; she was getting counseling, and so were the kids. Her husband, on the other hand, was in the living room watching television.

One day, Mary Ann came in to work and said, "I am going to get a divorce. It just hit me: We're all in counseling for a problem my husband has created, and he's not willing to do anything about it. Why are we trying to change who we are when we're okay? He's the one with the problem!" Then she said something profound: "I need to be aware of what I am teaching my kids about how to have a loving relationship. This isn't what I would want for them in their futures. I need to model for them how to take care of their needs and make positive changes for themselves."

What better example of modeling can we give others than to live a life of our choosing and our creation? By living our life fully, we show others that they can do it, too.

Exercise 5.4: An Open Invitation

Throw open your front door and invite your intentions and actions in for a conversation about your goals. Imagine that these two parts of yourself have taken on four-inch identities and are sitting on your shoulders, one on either side of your head. Listen closely to what they're saying and write down their conversation in your journal. What same old excuses do your actions use when they encounter obstacles in aligning with your intentions? How can your intentions support your actions, and vice versa? Consider the following example:

INTENTIONS: Let's open a dessert catering business in a year!

ACTIONS: That makes sense, especially since we did so well at the French Culinary Institute and attended several business courses at the City College.

INTENTIONS: I'm so glad we did that. I think one of our next steps is to ask our parents and grandparents to consider investing in our catering business.

ACTIONS: I would go along with that plan, but I don't think Dad's going to be too pleased. He might bring up how we failed to make a profit with our online antique business. Let's wait to make that call.

INTENTIONS: I hear your concern, but I really have a good feeling about running our own catering business. I think we can convince Dad and the others to help us out.

ACTIONS: Maybe you're right. Hey, why don't we work for someone who owns a catering business before we start our own business?

INTENTIONS: We've done that already and we learned a lot about how to avoid making mistakes.

ACTIONS: Did we learn all the mistakes we needed to learn about? I think we need to learn more before we dive into running our own catering business.

INTENTIONS: Okay, we'll do more research next week on the steps we need to take. Shall we also call the owner of the Good To Go catering business and set up a time to talk with him?

ACTIONS: That sounds like a plan. How about calling our Culinary Institute friends to tell them our exciting news? Maybe we can go out for drinks and celebrate.

INTENTIONS: That would be fun, but first, let's call our parents and set a time to meet with them to discuss borrowing money.

ACTIONS: I'm nervous about what they're going to say! Let's go out with our friends.

INTENTIONS: Okay, but before we call our friends, let's sit down and write out our strategy to ask Mom and Dad for a loan. Then we'll both feel better prepared to make the call.

ACTIONS: Great! Let's do that. I'll get the pen and paper.

As you can see, you are capable of aligning your intentions with your actions. It may take practice on your part to be clear about what you truly want and to muster the staying power to figure out how you're going to put those desires into action. Your excuses may stop by for occasional visits, as do ours, to remind you to assess where you are and what actions you are putting out to the world. It's not easy to face your fears and your past experiences of failure, but it is possible to do so. Taking another look at what you say you want and at what you are doing to create it is a great way to more clearly see the next step on your path toward goal achievement.

Doubts Happen

Another foe — and potential friend — in achieving your goals is your self-doubt. Doubts can be contagious. They won't necessarily kill you, but they might dampen your spirit, your sense of adventure, and your belief in yourself. If you're not careful about your doubts, you might unintentionally spread them to important people in your life.

Michelle's Story

I have long been plagued by a doubt about whether I have what it takes to be an accomplished artist. I haven't experienced failure as an artist per se; that would require me to put my artwork out into the world beyond my family and friends! What plagues me is the fear that I won't be taken seriously as an artist and that no one will like my artwork as much as my family, Goal Sister, and friends do. After all, I only doodle; I didn't go to art school, and I've never sold any of my creations. What makes me think I can succeed as an artist?

That said, living the life of an artist has always intrigued me. To get up every day and create art is my idea of heaven. I've imagined myself working in a studio filled with my knickknacks, somewhere out in nature, creating fabulous drawings, funky clothes, and fun everyday objects. I see myself easily filling orders and selling my artwork online and in women's catalogs. I've fantasized about getting together with artist friends, chatting about our latest endeavors, and encouraging each other's creative juices to flow. I've even imagined myself and my artwork being featured in a national magazine, and all the new connections I'd make and the wares I'd sell from this publicity. Oh, to be and live the life of an artist!

But then my self-doubt rudely yanks me back to what it views as "reality" by creating excuses ("I could start living the life of an artist if only I had more time to create art") and fears ("I don't want people to reject my artwork! That would hurt too much.") Talk about emotional muck! Yuck!

Thank goodness the important people in my life don't see my art that way. They all push me closer to living the life of an artist, countering my self-doubts and nudging me beyond my fears and excuses. Bart encourages me to create, and he's never questioned how much money I spend on art supplies or how much time I took to sew our guest-room curtains. Ann asked me to create her business-card graphics and to draw motivational images on her calendar pages.

My children are also hugely influential in helping me create my artwork. Zoë and Kanoa enjoy drawing with me, and they urge me to do creative work whenever I lose myself in my research work. They also remind me daily that, as the story about Ann's friend Mary Ann attests, actions speak louder than words; showing our children how I handle my doubts is the best way to teach them how to handle theirs. Furthermore, if I don't do what I say I'm going to do, Zoë and Kanoa are the first to call me on it. For example, when Zoë was twelve years old, she asked me why I wasn't creating art full-time. We had the following conversation:

MICHELLE: I'm working on putting my art out there.

ZOË: What do you mean?

MICHELLE: I'm not ready to be a full-blown artist yet.

ZOË: When will you be ready?

MICHELLE: That's a good question. I'm working on getting ready to be ready.

ZOË: Oh, what are you doing to get ready to be ready?

MICHELLE: I'm researching how to get into the greeting-card business. I'm drawing in my journal every day to get into the flow of creating. I'm doing Julia Cameron's twelve-step creative recovery program.

ZOË: Oh, now I get it. That's cool, Mom.

When she and her brother see me doing all these things, they learn that facing your doubts is a process. They learn that you have to stay engaged in that process, or else your dreams will fall by the wayside. Being a Goal Sister has helped me clarify how I want to face my doubts, and being Zoë and Kanoa's mom has helped me transform my doubts into desired actions.

The funny thing is, the more I allow myself to create because it's something I enjoy doing, the easier it becomes to loosen the grip on my self-imposed excuses and fears. This hasn't happened overnight, but it is happening. And don't get me wrong; my emotional muck hasn't completely left me. I still get pangs of "What are you thinking?" when I commit myself to drawing images for new projects. I recognize these pangs as signs of my emotional muck, thank them for their opinions, then go back to getting pleasure out of creating and putting it out there.

Doubts usually start as a light sprinkle: "I'm not sure I can do this. Can I handle this?" If someone questions your abilities or judgment, your doubts may turn into a drizzle. "I'm not the right person to do this! I'm going to blow it!" It can be difficult for some of us to hold back our downpour of doubts about our potential for success — especially if people we care about have doubted us at key points in our life.

Exercise 5.5: Let It Rain

Envision yourself standing under the awning of a building, holding out your hand to feel your doubts as they gently drizzle down on your success. Where did these doubts about yourself come from? What kinds of experiences did you have when you asked for advice or support from someone in the past? Has anyone important to you withheld support for any choices you made or for the direction you took with your life? What's been your experience with being accountable to someone close to you; were you dependable, reliable? Write about these experiences and the way they've affected how you see yourself as a Goal Sister.

When you're ready, take an umbrella of confidence, open it up, and use it to walk through your doubts. Where might you get this umbrella? Can you borrow it from another area of your life — one you feel confident about? Or maybe you can borrow the umbrella from someone you know who exudes confidence. That someone might be your Goal Sister. Go ahead, she won't mind your borrowing it. As you read over your past experiences of doubt, open your umbrella and hold it up to these experiences. Notice your grip on the umbrella. Notice how dry and safe you are underneath your umbrella. Write about those feelings in your journal.

Will She or Won't She?

When you're all alone and facing your goals, part of you may find yourself doubting your Goal Sister's willingness to participate in supporting you and your desired life. You may use your initial doubts about the process as a way to justify a lower expectation of your Goal Sister. "She has two kids; that keeps her so busy!" or "She might think I can't get it together on my own and that she'll have to carry me along." Take these thoughts and toss them out an open window! "Sure, Ann! No problem, Michelle!" you think to yourself. We hear your sarcasm, and we understand it. In fact, we encourage it.

Sarcasm and cynicism are real. So are your goals and dreams. As Gemini women, we have both had many conversations about duality. You don't have to be a Gemini to understand the concept behind yin and yang, hot and cold, up and down. We don't want to trivialize your feelings, but remember that there's always the choice of an opposite reaction. Our doubts can be overcome.

As you mull over that thought, you may find yourself wondering, "How? Surely if it were that simple, I would have already done it." Well, dear Goal Sister, no one said it would be easy. The process involves courage, willingness, and acceptance. Chances are that the strength to face your doubts is already within you.

Goal Sister Group Story

Karen, one of our group members, was ready to change her life. A manager of a corporate office, she wanted to do something totally different: massage therapy! She enrolled in a school and took classes every other weekend. She loved learning and practicing massage, and she felt a pull to use it to help people cope with pain and other physical challenges.

At Goal Sister meetings, Karen would seek input regarding when to leave her job and how to get a massage business going. She was hesitant to leave the financial security of the job, yet eager to begin her new life. In true Goal Sister fashion, the other members gently reminded her of the reasons why she wanted to leave her employer. Every time, she would respond with "Yes, but...." Over a four-month period, however, her tune changed to "I want to do this now. I have studied hard, I have prepared myself for the change, and I can do it."

Karen declared her intention to be a massage therapist by ordering a massage therapy T-shirt and wearing it in the weeks leading up to graduation. This affirmed her goal and told the world that she was serious about her stated vision. She ordered business cards and interviewed other massage therapists to check out new techniques. She hosted a dinner for professional women to brainstorm business details, such as what the massage room might look like and how she might provide optimal customer service. She designed a marketing plan that spelled out the number of clients she wanted and the number of hours per day she wanted to work. Then she opened her business.

Karen has done well in her first year as a massage therapist. Like all of us, she has doubts. Her doubts aren't so much about whether she made the right decision as they are about her own talents. But she is learning to trust her gifts, toss out marketing ideas that don't excite her, and focus on the skills and caring attitude that make her massage therapy office a place that attracts people seeking caring, healing, and pain relief. She looks back on her former life as a manager and has no regrets about leaving. "That tells me a lot," she says.

You've taken the time to find courage to confront your doubts. Congratulate yourself for that big step, and affirm your willingness to move forward. Willingness requires that you be open to sharing it all with your Goal Sister. It requires that you take the steps necessary to have what you say you want. It involves doing that not just for yourself, but for your Goal Sister as well. This may sound stringent and forceful; if you respond to it that way, it can be. But it can also be fluid and natural. You and your Goal Sister will be able to discuss your level of willingness to engage in this process. We encourage you to utilize the following continuum to identify your current level of readiness. When you meet with your Goal Sister, be honest with her about your expectations and discuss your benchmarks of progress together.

Exercise 5.6: The Continuum

Review the following statements and circle the number that best represents your level of willingness to participate in this process:

1. I'm interested in learning more about the Goal Sister process.

2. I'd like to have a couple of good ideas from my Goal Sister.

3. I know some specific goals I'd like to work on with my Goal Sister.

4. I'm willing to share my goals and dreams with my Goal Sister.

5. I'm ready to explore all the ways in which I can achieve my goals.

6. I'm excited about giving support to my Goal Sister, and about knowing that it will come back to me as well.

7. I'm open to hearing my Goal Sister's ideas about achieving my goals, and I believe that having someone to brainstorm solutions with will be beneficial.

8. I'd like my Goal Sister to help me achieve half of my goals and dreams.

9. I'm prepared to have my Goal Sister's support in achieving 85 percent of my goals.

10. I expect to obtain all of my goals, and I believe that my Goal Sister and I will be amazed and thrilled with what we will accomplish together.

No matter which number you circled, ask yourself what it will take to move up to the next one. What support do you need in order to do that? What feedback are you looking for? How do you want to be there for your Goal Sister? You'll have the opportunity to explore these questions later with your Goal Sister, but begin now to consider your initial thoughts.

The last part of this identification process is to accept where you are right now. While you may be excited to be in a new Goal Sister friendship, enthusiastic about having her support, and energized about moving forward with your life, you may still feel some hesitancy — and more doubts. Pay attention to them. While it may not be easy to release your doubts and hesitation just yet, we suggest that you start acting as if it were possible.

Believe that now is your time to create the life you desire. Believe that you deserve the support and feedback of a like-minded woman who understands your challenges as well as she understands her own. Trust that this form of support will move you gently forward to all that you desire. Accept the benefits that are to come. You have been heard. Your desires are now coming into manifestation. Accept this as true and move forward!

Chapter 5 Summary

★ Putting your needs before those of others may set off an excuse-making alarm: "I have no time to take care of my needs" or "After I make this deadline, I can focus on me." But you can learn to give self-care a valuable place in your life.

★ Recognize that your doubts and fears might arise as you work through the Goal Sister process. It's important to stay focused on your desired outcomes and not become overwhelmed. Ask your Goal Sister for help in moving past your doubts and fears.

★ For some of us, the more failures we've had with elusive goals in the past, the more quickly we give up on ourselves. These experiences may have crystallized into limiting beliefs that affect your goal-achievement efforts.

★ It may be difficult to align your words with your actions when it means facing your fear of failure, success, or rejection. Pay attention to times when your words and actions are out of sync and move toward aligning them.

★ You may also experience self-doubt as you work toward your goals. Pay attention to your doubts and their origins. Talk with your Goal Sister about how she has faced her doubts, and share your own triumphs with her.

Questions

★ *What is your biggest fear in relation to achieving your goals?*

★ *What steps can you take this week to face your fear so that it doesn't overwhelm you and your goal achievement efforts?*

Chapter 6

How Does Your
Goal Garden Grow?

T ake a deep breath, Goal Sister, and pat yourself on the back. You've done a lot of work to get to this stage of the process. You've selected your priority goals. You've shared and discussed your goals with your Goal Sister. You've survived visits from your fears and doubts. So, please take a moment to relax, refuel, and rest your eyes. Let go of any lingering stress, and clear your mind for a stroll down the path to your future.

As you stroll, notice the flower gardens lining your path. There are flower gardens of family, friends, creativity, and play on your left, and flower gardens of spirituality, significant other, and health on your right. Just around the bend, you can see the career/job, money, and volunteer service flowers, with the environment flowers growing right beside them. You've found the flower gardens of your goal categories along your path of life.

Which of your flower gardens need to be tended now? Which ones need watering? Which ones are fine in the shade, left to grow at their own pace? Which flower gardens are overrun with weeds? How you choose to tend to your goal gardens depends on the type of flowers you want to plant, the extent of your gardening plans, how much time and effort you have to nurture your flowers, your gardening gear, and where you are right now in life. Take another deep breath, Goal Sister. It's time to tend your flower gardens!

This is your garden path, and your Goal Sister has her own path. Your commitment to your Goal Sister friendship means that you are willing to develop yourself and your garden while sharing your gardening wisdom with her, just as she's developing herself and her own garden. Along the way, you'll rake out marvelous rows of support, motivation, and accountability. Until then, we suggest that you take a personal inventory of your plans and resources before you begin cultivating your own soil and pulling your own weeds.

Personal Inventory

Your gardening efforts are sure to reap great rewards if you include the following five factors in your personal inventory:

1. Starting your Garden Journal
2. Gathering your gardening tools
3. Tilling the soil
4. Harnessing the sunlight
5. Setting up your garden shed

Your Garden Journal

Until now, your journal has been an important part of your goal-setting efforts; it's been a place for you to record your thoughts and responses to the exercises in this book. Now your journal is poised to become your Garden Journal. Just as gardeners record changes in growing patterns, you will track the points along your garden path that represent personal growth. When you achieve a goal in an unexpected way or someone notices changes in your attitudes and actions, record that event or insight in your journal. Whether you feel deflated, elated, or frustrated about your progress, write your feelings and thoughts in your Garden Journal. Feel free to draw or glue pictures of yourself in your journal. Becoming aware of your growing patterns is one way to improve your gardening skills.

Exercise 6.1: Getting Down and Dirty with Your Goals

Get out your journal and look over the goals you committed to working on at your last Goal Sister meeting. Notice which of your goals are Large, which are Medium, and which are Small. For each of your priority goals, write the following statement at the top of a new page and complete it:

I, [your name], commit to working on "[your priority goal]" over the next [choose one: week, month, or three months].

Under each commitment, write your expectations related to its achievement. For instance, what are your hopes around planting and growing your goals? Do you anticipate your experience to be like slogging through the mud or swinging from the vines? How do you plan to communicate with your Goal Sister about your progress — through phone calls, e-mails, in-person meetings? If you encounter challenges, how will you share them with your Goal Sister, and will you ask her for help? Write about your expectations before you proceed.

Preparing Your Gardening Tools

To achieve the best possible results, you need to get your garden tools in shape or acquire new ones. By "tools" we mean anything that enhances your efforts to work on your goals. Depending on your priority goals, your tools can range from workout clothes to a daily planner to a CD player. Maybe you need new glasses or contact lenses; when was the last time you had your eyes checked? If you're like us, your computer is a vital tool. Do you need to get a new Internet service provider or buy software upgrades? How's your desk chair? Do your neck and shoulders ache when you sit for too long? Your library card might be another tool. Do you need to renew it or pay off outstanding fines? You may need additional tools as you work toward your goals.

Additional Essential Tools

If you're like most goal gardeners, you'll want a complete arsenal of tools at your disposal. Consider adding the following garden gear to your collection of tools:

- A HOE: Your "hoe" will be the actions you take to clear a space for new plants or to give existing goal flowers more room to grow. You might also use your hoe to unearth roots of old problems that haven't been dug out of your garden. If left unchecked, old roots can slow the growth of your new goal flowers.

- WEEDING TOOLS: Like your hoe, you may use your weeding tools to get rid of unwanted plants or distractions that can crowd out your efforts to successfully nurture your goal flowers. We suggest that you dig out your weeds instead of spraying them with weed-killer; it's better for the environment, and you're more likely to get to the root of the problem.

- HOSE, SPRINKLER, AND WATERING CAN: Your goal plants depend on being watered with the appropriate amounts of encouragement and support. Use a watering can with young goal plants to gently infuse them with support. Once your goal plants are established and they don't require your full attention, you might want to use a sprinkler. Sometimes your Goal Sister may lend a helping hand by watering your goal flowers with her sprinkler!

Preparing Your Soil

No matter what flower goals you plant and how well you care for them, you will get meager results if your soil is in poor condition. We define "soil" as your thoughts and beliefs as they relate to achieving your goals. Take a minute to think about your beliefs about meeting your goals. How's your topsoil — the rich, healthy thoughts you have about meeting your goals? Is it intact or did it blow away during a particularly stressful year? How is the quality of your thoughts and beliefs? Longtime gardeners recommend testing your soil before you improve it. Fortunately, you don't need to purchase a fancy soil test kit to do that.

Exercise 6.2: Testing Your Soil

To get ready for your soil test, take out your journal and write "My Beliefs and Thoughts about Being Successful" at the top of a new page. Ask yourself the following questions:

- What are my beliefs about my ability to grow a vibrant, beautiful goal garden? Do I believe that I have the stamina and commitment to work on my goals? Can I see myself achieving my goals?

- Which of my beliefs are rich in optimism and confidence, and which are acidic in pessimism and skepticism?

- What steps can I take to nurture my optimism and confidence, and release my pessimism and skepticism?

Take some time to consider these questions, then write your responses.

After you've finished, read through what you've written. As the master gardener of your life, you have the choice to give power to your beliefs and thoughts. For example, you can choose to harness your confidence in one area of your life and transfer it to another area. You can also choose to surrender to your pessimism and doubts, which will impede your progress. Be aware of those temptations and resist having a knee-jerk reaction to your acidic beliefs. You can also choose to compost your acidic beliefs and thoughts and turn this waste into healthy, beneficial beliefs and thoughts. Chapter 7 shows you how to identify and reframe your limiting beliefs, and chapter 8 describes how your Goal Sister can help you use your beliefs to enrich your goal achievement efforts.

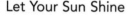

Let Your Sun Shine

Like most flowers, your goal flowers will need their share of sunlight. Your time, your energy, and your commitment are the most important sources of sunlight for your goals. Consequently, it is essential that you continue to carve out time for yourself and manage any clouds of distraction that might take your attention away from working on your goals. We know, we know — easier said than done! But we wouldn't dwell on this point unless it was important. As much as you can, keep "take care of me" among your top three priorities. Putting yourself first will go a long way toward growing the goal garden you desire.

Extra Nudging

While you are the primary source of sunlight for your goals, support from your Goal Sister and other people will boost your abilities to shine. Don't forget to thank them for contributing to your light. The cumulative effect of all this sunshine makes for a bright outlook on your goals.

You and Your Garden Shed

Your planting endeavor won't be possible without a garden shed to support you. By "garden shed" we mean the place in your home that you can call your own — a place where you can do a lot of your thinking and planning. We've each worked toward our goals in a number of places, but our home offices have served as our primary garden sheds. We've dedicated a lot of effort to making these spaces conducive to accomplishing our goals.

Michelle's Story

My home office has evolved over time along with me. The heart of my office is a beat-up solid walnut desk that my husband and I bought years ago at a Salvation Army store in Chicago. We paid twenty-five dollars for the desk — and fifty dollars for the movers to haul it up four flights of stairs! The desk moved with us over the years, much to the chagrin of various movers. I've had a variety of desk chairs, each more ergonomically correct than the previous one. As I went from full-time employment to self-employment to telecommuting part-time, I purchased computers, printers, scanners, and lots of software. I've always had an assortment of filing cabinets, printer cabinets, tables, and bookcases.

Finding the ideal place for my office hasn't always been easy. When we lived in a basement apartment in Bloomington, Illinois, the desk was in the corner of our living room — which also functioned as a speedway for my then-two-year-old daughter, Zoë. Not much work got done there. Moving into our first house allowed us to spread out; there, my office was in our basement, sandwiched between the laundry room and the kids' playroom. I had a great setup: My computer and printers were within arm's reach; a bulletin board hung over my desk, cluttered with my kids' drawings, photos of friends and family, and thank-you cards; my favorite Frida Kahlo, Brian Andreas, and Jane Evershed prints hung on the walls alongside my framed diplomas; six bookcases, filled with business books on one side and children's books on the other, stood back-to-back and served as a barrier between me and SpongeBob. An added

*bonus was being able to hear when the kids needed my atten-
tion or when it was time to put softener into the washing
machine.*

*Before we moved to Hawaii, we lightened our load by
recycling eleven file boxes full of office paper. Much of the stuff
from my Bloomington home office is in my Hawaii office, but
now it's all aboveground and adjacent to the master bedroom.
I have a view of our backyard, with plenty of light and a
breeze coming through the open windows. My office is sepa-
rated from the rest of the house, affording me much-needed
peace and quiet.*

Ann's Story

*When I began my own business, it was important to me that
my home office reflect my energy and passion for my new
work. It also had to be "me." I didn't want it to look like a
"professional work area" designed to please clients. Most of my
work is done over the phone anyway, so that concern became
moot early on.*

*I found a bleached pine desk and credenza that suited my
desire for a light feeling. And I discovered a great long worktable
that has seen better days — perfect for gluing and drawing on
when I create Michelle's calendar pages. I had one side of the
worktable shaved a bit so that it would fit in the allotted space,
but that was a minor detail. My bookshelves hold my paper supplies, resource notebooks, and marketing packets. The phone and
fax are nearby and, of course, my wonderful computer is always
ready for a creative venture. There's a tabletop fountain that
calms me in the midst of working on a deadline, and I always
light a candle to honor the creative flow when I work.*

*Most of all, I like the way the space feels. It's relaxed, yet
efficient. I joke with my friends that they're walking into the
World Headquarters of Ann Leach Life Coaching. I think big
that way, and I have the "extras" in the office to support me
in that vision.*

On the walls of my office are motivational sayings and cards that Michelle and others have given me. The bumper stickers on the bulletin board remind me "Do Your Dream" and "Living My Vision." On the windowsill in front of me is my picture gallery of support people, including Michelle, the original Goal Sisters group, my prayer partners, and my friends Ted, Nancy, and Faith. There's also an eight-by-ten-inch picture of Jesus laughing, to remind me that I have powerful business partners who want the best for me — and to remind me to lighten up on myself! Jesus is right next to the Jane Evershed print "Leap of Faith." Another piece of artwork perfectly represents who I am as a life coach: Mary Engelbreit's print of a little girl holding a bowlful of slips of paper that read "Lives," and the title saying "Get One." My Kauai calendar was a gift from MJ, and it helps me think of Michelle and MJ every day. The whiteboard with a flowchart of my current volunteer service goals keeps my vision before me. All the motivational posters and affirmations have a positive effect on me.

Our garden shed and how it supports us are important. We each feel fortunate to have the luxury of a whole room to call ours, but we know that's not always feasible. We urge you to get creative about how you approach carving out a space in your home to call your own. Whether that space is your kitchen, a spare bedroom, or a corner of the master bedroom, making it yours will help you feel more focused and energized.

Exercise 6.3: Designing Your Garden Shed

Where do you want to build your garden shed? If your space isn't completely set up for you to work on achieving your goals, how can you make it more comfortable, more conducive to reaching your goals, and more representative of you and your dreams? Go to this place now with your journal and jot down some notes on how you can prepare it for your gardening endeavors. Here's an example of what your list might look like:

HOME OFFICE

1. Organize the piles of paper on my desk.
2. Get a recycling bin for my office paper.
3. Put away the files, papers, and books I'm not currently using.
4. Install new software on my computer.

LIVING ROOM

1. Personalize the left corner of the couch as my own.
    a. Keep pens and journal nearby.
    b. Make sure the lamp extends to that area.
2. Announce my plans to my family.
3. Create a new morning planning ritual there.

Now, instead of closing up your journal and doing nothing, set it down and do at least three of the things on your list. After that, consider creating additional priority goals from the rest of your notes.

~~~~~~~

Depending on your situation, it may be more feasible for you to use spaces outside your home as your garden shed. If you don't need to be "plugged in," a park, sculpture garden, or hotel lobby may be an option. Otherwise, you might consider libraries, a friend's home, or any of the places where you've held Goal Sister meetings.

You've accomplished many items on your personal inventory. Nice work, Goal Sister! As you grow your goal garden, you may need to upgrade your gardening gear, maintain your soil cultivation efforts (don't forget to record any insights or experiences in your Garden Journal!), continue nurturing yourself so that your rays of energy and commitment shine through, and persist in making your garden shed yours. You are more than ready to start working in your goal garden.

Starting Here, Starting Now

Where should you start? We recommend starting with the smallest flower beds you have committed to growing. We want you to be successful with your initial gardening efforts — and inspired to make room in your life to grow more gardens! So whether you direct your initial efforts to seeding a new idea or trying again with seeds that didn't bloom in the past, it's time to plant those small gardens. Be on the lookout, though, for thorny issues and pesky bugs!

Starting Small

Planting new ideas and actions is an exciting prospect. Make sure you have your optimistic beliefs (rich soil) and a watering can. Consider the various places available for planting your Small Goals: in a pot or container, in the corner of a new goal-category garden, or among other goal flowers in your established goal-category garden. Where you plant your goal seedling depends on your comfort level. For example, if your Small Goal is "spend thirty minutes a day reading for pleasure," and it's one of many activities you currently do under your "creativity and play" goal category, then you'll probably clear a space for this new seed to grow among your other goal flowers in that category. However, if this Small Goal is the first one to be planted in your "creativity and play" goal garden, you may want to first seed your actions in a contained way and pay more attention to nurturing this new plant until you have successfully met this goal for a week or longer.

Once you begin attaining success with your Small Goals, you may be ready to plant and nurture more Small Goals that will lead to achieving a Medium Goal. You have the same planting options to consider as you did with your first Small Goal. Starting more goal seedlings and maintaining several simultaneously will probably require more of your time and energy. We have faith that you can do it, and so does your Goal Sister. Give her a call and talk about how to pace yourself and harness the energy and enthusiasm you may have gained from your initial successes. Don't forget to write about your progress and your insights in your Garden Journal.

Revisiting Old Habits

Achieving certain Medium Goals may require more of your attention, care, and patience. Goals like "decrease my cigarette smoking" and "stop putting off unpleasant tasks" are two examples that come to mind. Like us, you may have had poor results with past attempts at changing old habits. These can be the toughest goals to revisit and reattempt.

Michelle's Story

I bite my fingernails. It's a habit I've had since I was a young girl. I bite my nails when I'm stressed out, when I'm bored, and during scary parts of movies. I've tried to kick my nail-biting habit by polishing my nails and by dipping my fingertips in hot sauce. Neither of those efforts succeeded. I've tried to bite other things instead of my nails, and ended up having lots of chewed-up pens and pencils. It's not a habit I'm proud of.

I've been successful twice in my life at reducing my nail-biting. The first time was when my children were infants and I changed a lot of diapers (yuck!). The second time was about a year ago after I listened to a recorded phone message based on

classical conditioning theory (www.psychresearch.com/nails.html).
Both times I stopped biting my nails for months; both times I later
reverted to biting my nails. Why? I'm not sure. I do know that I
am committed to including "stop biting my fingernails" as one of
my priority goals after I finish writing this book. Who knows?
This next effort might be the one that sticks.

If one of your Medium Goals is to change an old habit, we applaud you. We know it's not easy to give up persistent habits, and we're glad you're taking this opportunity to have a different outcome. We consider these goal flowers to be our roses; we admire them in someone else's yard, they represent thorny issues for us, and they need a lot of ongoing attention. We understand that working toward these goals may require you to develop new coping responses to stress, which is an additional commitment you have to make. In this case, your new coping responses must be nurtured in addition to changing the habit itself. We suggest looking at how you can increase your level of sunshine, and perhaps getting professional help in learning new coping responses.

Garden Pests

Have you noticed that when you tend to certain goal flowers, you become bombarded with unsupportive comments from pesky friends, family members, and colleagues? We playfully refer to these people as "bugs." They may sting you with their criticisms ("That's not going to work") or eat a hole in your confidence ("What makes you think you're going to succeed this time?"). Ouch! Sometimes the bugs don't say anything about the noticeable progress you're making because they're so focused on bugging you. Whatever the case, there are several ways to deal with pesky bugs:

- Ignore them and hope they go away
- Avoid them when you're feeling vulnerable
- Ask them to keep their stinging remarks to themselves

We know it's a bug's life. We just wish they would stop bugging *us!*

Upkeep and Minor Repairs

Not all current goal-related efforts require planting seeds. If you previously worked toward a goal and had some success with it, but have neglected to tend it for a while, you may want to do some maintenance gardening. Parts of your goal garden may be overrun with weeds, or there may be dry spots. Sometimes new problems sprout up, and it's important to nip them in the bud before they grow into old, unwieldy problems. To get the established but neglected areas of your goal garden to flourish, you might work on them several times each week or whenever you get the chance. The intention of your efforts is to preserve and nurture these areas of your life.

Michelle's Story

After accomplishing many business goals related to initiating and running my program-evaluation consulting business, I began to work on my spiritual goals. I devoured books like Everyday Sacred *by Sue Bender and* Everyday Zen *by Charlotte Joko Beck. I felt more centered, and I wanted to practice mindfulness daily. It was easier to do that when I was immersed in daily meditation. When I got busy with raising my children and running my business, my daily meditations fell by the wayside, as did my focus on living from my intentions.*

Then my mom sent me a "Live Aloha" bumper sticker. My family and I were still living in Bloomington, and the thought of spreading aloha to my fellow drivers intrigued me. "Hmmm," I thought, "maybe this will help me live my intention of treating others with respect and kindness." I stuck it on the back bumper of my minivan. Every time I got on the road, my "Live Aloha" bumper sticker reminded me that cutting someone off or gesturing at fellow drivers with my fist didn't evoke the aloha spirit. It reminded me not to accelerate at a yellow light. It reminded me that the road rage I perfected while living in Chicago in the eighties isn't a desirable behavior. My bumper sticker helped me become a kinder and gentler driver!

There were times, though, when I felt road rage creeping up inside me — like the day when I was late for an appointment on the other side of town, caught every red light between home and my destination, and got trapped behind every slow driver on the road (what are the odds of that happening?!). That's when I found myself becoming super-impatient. But before my hand pounded on the horn and I started weaving in and out of traffic, I took a deep breath and remembered that my "Live Aloha" sticker was telling all the drivers behind me that I support mutual respect and kindness. Talk about putting the brakes on my anger! Whew! As I transformed back into the mild-mannered driver I intended to be, I allowed the next pushy driver to take my space in traffic, slowed to a stop at the next yellow light, and encouraged pedestrians to cross the street in front of me. After all, who did I truly want to be: someone who used the aloha spirit only as a pretty bumper sticker, or someone whose driving embodied the aloha spirit?

Doing upkeep with your goals means doing whatever it takes to keep up an area of your goal garden or attend to new problems before they become full-grown weeds.

Cultivating Your Style

When you're ready to undertake several Medium Goals or a Large Goal, it's time for you to consider your cultivation style. Just as you and your Goal Sister have your own garden paths to walk, you may have your own approaches to working on your goals. Do you prefer to outline all the steps involved in your plan, then work on those steps sequentially? Or do you prefer to envision your completed goal, get an idea of the steps involved, then feel more inclined to start with a small step and see where it leads you? Knowing those preferences will give you a better understanding of the time and effort you'll need to meet your goals. Your Goal Sister will also benefit from knowing your preferences as she supports you in your planting and growing efforts.

There is no right or wrong style for working on your goals. Your comfort level, experiences, and skills will influence whether you stick with one approach, experiment with others, or use a combination of approaches.

Surveying the Landscape

You might prefer to outline the steps that will lead to your goals before you swing into action. This involves envisioning your completed goal garden first, then planning the steps to make it come to life. This big-picture approach is especially helpful if you're more comfortable with taking steps sequentially toward a known destination. It is also helpful if you have a lot of choices and important decisions to make along the way, because it offers a systematic way to consider your options. For example, if you're planning your wedding, you might feel more comfortable sitting down with your life-partner-to-be and planning all the specific steps you need to take to have the wedding of your dreams. You might take on some steps separately ("I'll arrange the flowers and you make the car arrangements") and do some of them together ("Let's both select the reception menu and music"). Once you put these steps into an anticipated order, you'll both know ahead of time that a certain step here will lead to taking a certain step there. Having an outline of the big picture is comforting for people who like to work toward their goals one identified step at a time while keeping the entire project in mind.

One Plot at a Time

If outlining the big picture first doesn't fit with your style, it might be because you prefer to work on your goal garden in a piecemeal fashion, trusting that your efforts will eventually come together in a satisfying way that matches your visualization of your accomplished goal. This approach tends to be more fluid. It involves immersing yourself in new experiences and, based on these encounters, figuring out what your next steps toward achieving your goal will be. It relies on your ability to remain present, listening to your inner self and following through on its guidance. The following story is an example of taking a piecemeal approach to achieving your goals.

Michelle's Story

A few years into our Goal Sister friendship, my artistic goals consistently appeared on my priority list. Ann and I talked about them during in-person meetings, and when Ann moved to Missouri, we talked about them over the phone or via Instant Messages on our computers. I remained serious in my intentions to work toward my artistic goals, but that didn't necessarily show up in my actions.

Ann and I continued having phone contact and Instant-Message communications about my artistic goals after I moved to Hawaii in 2002. Being back home inspired me to get serious about creating artwork. I called Ann and told her so. I didn't have specific plans, but I knew that I had to find my muse. One Friday night, when my family and I were at a favorite bookstore, I walked down the self-help aisle and spotted a book with a beautiful black-and-white photograph of a waterfall on its cover. I took the book off the shelf. It was The Widening Stream: The Seven Stages of Creativity, *by David Ulrich. As I flipped through the pages, I remembered having seen the author's name before. Something told me I had to buy the book, so I did.*

When we got home, I rummaged through the stuff on my desk and found a glossy flyer from the Honolulu Academy of Arts. David Ulrich was teaching a class on creativity the next day! Realizing how remarkable it was for me to have spotted David's book the day before his workshop inspired me to take his class. It was too late in the evening to call and register, so I got to the class early the next morning — only to find that it was full. David agreed to let me join the class anyway. It was an awesome experience, and it inspired me to get back into drawing. My muse stayed with me for about six months; then I let other things take precedence over my artwork and she went away.

One Saturday night, when my family and I were at another bookstore (we like bookstores!), I was checking out the bargain books and came upon Julia Cameron's The Artist's Way. *I'd heard of the book and it looked interesting, so I bought it and promptly put it on the shelf. Two months went by.*

In the midst of writing this book, I hit a huge creative block. I kicked myself for not treating my muse better. In my haste to find a self-help business book on my shelf, I found The Artist's Way *— or maybe it found me! I glanced at the first couple of pages, and something about it spoke to me; I decided to follow the program set forth in* The Artist's Way. *During the sixth week of the program, my muse returned and put an end to my creative block. Reading this inspirational book, writing my morning pages (one of the exercises in the book), and taking my inner artist on dates really worked! I'm grateful that my muse has taken up residence with me again.*

As Michelle's story illustrates, one benefit of using the piecemeal approach is being more open to experiencing serendipitous occurrences along the way and perhaps having more flexibility about incorporating them into your steps toward goal achievement.

The "To and Fro" Style

We recommend that you try the "to and fro" style when tending multiple goal gardens. Seasoned gardeners use this technique because they realize that their gardens are in different stages of growth and often need different kinds of attention on any given day. For example, you may want to first survey your "family and friends" goal garden and figure out what resources you want to put into improving these relationships before identifying and taking smaller steps toward achieving those goals. At the same time, you might start doing some light weeding on the "job/career" garden, putting out feelers for new job opportunities in another department. Then your focus might shift toward the dry patch in your "significant other" area. While there, you'll be so close to your "family and friends" garden that you might as well water that corner of your life, too. And you can just reach your "creativity and play" goal flowers from there, so you might spend an afternoon relaxing to your favorite music.

Like your life, there's no right or wrong way to tend your goal gardens. The more experience you get with working on multiple goals across different goal categories, the more comfortable you'll get at balancing your focus, time, and efforts.

Major Planting

When you're interested in changing significant areas of your life, you're ready to undertake major work in one or more of your goal gardens. There are several ways to accomplish this.

Transplanting Your Skills

Perhaps you have an established goal garden that's been blooming beautifully for years. Many people have admired your garden, and you're proud of the work you've done to get it to this point. Recently, though, you've noticed that the blooms aren't as vibrant as they once were, or that certain goal flower varieties have overtaken areas of your garden. Whether it's your "significant other" garden or your "job/career" garden, it might be time to clear out the old growth by transplanting the best of your established efforts into newer parts of this garden.

Michelle's Story

I met my friend Sarah about five years ago. At that point, she was working as a special-education teacher at a small rural elementary school. Sarah was perfect for the job! She was a self-starter, she worked well with the other teachers, and she really blossomed when it came to teaching her behaviorally disabled students. Sarah also excelled at developing fun learning games. But while she enjoyed her job and her students, she didn't get along with her supervisor, who undervalued her knowledge and skills and constantly undercut her efforts.

One day, Sarah told me that she wanted to develop and sell her educational games. I shared my experiences of running a solo business and directed her to helpful books and online resources. Being a single mom, Sarah needed to carefully consider her steps before heading out on her own. She contacted a few suppliers and made connections with a professor who was interested in being part of her new project.

Sarah's situation with her supervisor became unbearable. She left her full-time job and began substitute-teaching, giving up the financial security of a consistent paycheck and benefits. But her belief in her own potential was stronger than the risk.

Within a year of leaving her full-time job, Sarah told me that she was postponing the launch of her educational game business. She was still enthusiastic about the idea, but she realized that she couldn't financially afford to do it now and that it would take too much time away from her relationship with her daughter. I admired her for making the right decision for her and her daughter.

Sarah called recently to tell me about her new full-time position as a special-education coordinator. She was courted by several district administrators who knew of her talents and skills. Sarah is excited about all the possibilities of this new venture.

Like Sarah, you may encounter resistance or endure temporary setbacks before you reap the rewards of starting anew. But you may also find, like Sarah, that when one route doesn't pan out, there may be other interesting paths to explore.

Planting a Whole New Garden

Let's say that you're interested in designing, planting, and growing a whole new garden. As you visualize this garden, you might imagine several seasons of goal flowers blooming in the same golden and orange hues: yellow daisies in the spring followed by brown-eyed Susans and daylilies in the summer, with marigolds and mums lasting into the fall. What about planting some annuals around the perimeter? How about new bushes and trees alongside your goal garden to balance the colors and shield your goal flowers from the wind? You might want to add a birdbath or make a sculpture for a climbing vine. As your vision expands, you become more and more excited.

Planting and maintaining such a large garden is similar to working on a Large Goal, which takes up most, if not all, of a single goal category and will require sustained excitement and constant effort. For example, the goal "get an MBA" clearly involves a lot of steps. You might map out your strategy and include specific timelines and tasks to accomplish. You might spend a lot of time researching your options. Going to the library and checking out various resources, as well as visiting bookstores to buy current books on test-taking and getting into graduate school, will definitely make your list of things to do. You might look at school Websites and get information about their programs. Maybe you'll seek advice from recent graduates, or set up appointments to talk with professors and graduate students at the schools you're interested in.

Achieving Large Goals often requires extensive planning, information gathering, and decision making. It also involves simultaneous efforts in other goal categories. Using the "get an MBA" example, you may need to save extra money or apply for student loans to pay your tuition (money goals), and it will benefit you to increase your self-care during stressful times and continue exercising (health goals). Working on a Large Goal requires patience, ongoing efforts in multiple goal categories, and sustained vision.

Dig In, Sister!

If you're working on a Medium Goal or a Large Goal, chances are you'll need to dig for information and store it somewhere. It's important to consider what information to dig for, where to dig for it, and how to store the information you uncover.

What to Dig For

Your purpose in digging is twofold: to increase your knowledge and understanding about a specific goal you're interested in, and to learn about the different approaches you can take to achieve that goal. Gathering information will increase your knowledge about what you must do to achieve your goals, including the skills and experiences you'll need.

Ann's Story

Back in 1997, when I first entertained the idea of moving from counseling to coaching as a profession, I knew I needed some specific information. For example, what were the distinctions between the two? What kind of liability issues were there for coaches? Was it necessary to be certified? Given that I already had some great skills, did I need to attend a training program? To find answers, I devised a plan.

First I visited the International Coach Federation Website. There, I found articles about coaching and a database of coaches who were ready to help clients with a variety of needs. I made it my goal to read the material and interview five coaches about their training and business experiences within a particular time period. That done, I moved on to checking out training programs. Each day, I visited one training school's Website and scheduled an informational telephone interview with them for the following week.

Taking these small steps gave me the time I needed to absorb what I was learning. And it was fun to look forward to accomplishing something each day toward my goal of a career shift.

Once I committed to being a coach, I began reading books about starting a business. I even found two books geared specifically toward building a coaching practice. The coaching community turned out to be highly supportive, so it was no problem to ask other coaches to share sample client contracts and marketing materials. They did so willingly, which freed up a lot of time for me to work on other aspects of my business development. It also reminded me that reaching out and asking for help works!

Exercise 6.4: Exploring New Territory

Embark on an information search that's a little risky for you, whether that means joining a new association and attending their meetings or talking to someone in person about your interests. Go ahead! You have nothing to lose but your fears and doubts. Write in your journal about your experiences so you can share them with your Goal Sister later.

Where to Dig

The possibilities of where to find information are limitless. We encourage you to open yourself to everything that can help you achieve your goals. It doesn't matter *where* you start; it matters *that* you start. So go ahead and read local, regional, and national newspapers and magazines. Talk to people who are doing what you want to do. Peruse the library and bookstores for books that might jump-start your imagination and knowledge. Read self-help books, do the exercises in them, and record your experiences. Search Amazon.com and other online bookstores. Watch talk shows to get information or gain new insights. Surf the Internet for relevant Websites. Attend classes and seminars to round out what you already know. All of this information gathering will lead you to greater understanding, knowledge, and experience that you can apply toward achieving your goals.

How to Organize Your Information

It's important to create a system for storing the information you find in your digging. We suggest that you keep your information in file folders labeled by goal categories (job/career, health, and so on). Similarly, store the information you access via the Internet in a Goal Sister file in your Favorites list or in file folders in your main Goal Sister folder. Taking the extra time now to organize your paper and computer storage system will go a long way toward keeping you on top of the information you collect.

Exercise 6.5: Storing Your Information

Start a notebook, file drawer, or folder for your goals, and collect all of your information in one place. Don't let the magazine articles, newspaper clippings, and loose paper pile up! Store it now.

Working in Your Garden

As you undertake your planting efforts, we encourage you to maintain communication with your Goal Sister about your plans, decision points, and the results of your efforts. Your efforts will inspire her to work hard toward her goals, too.

Goal Sister Group Story

Toward the end of the original eight-week Goal Sister Group pilot program, MJ decided to realize her dreams in a big way. Newly divorced, she was ready to be healed and to create a new life for herself. Hawaii had been her favorite travel destination for years. At one of our meetings, she said, "You guys, I love Hawaii so much I would live there if I could!" Over the next few weeks, she made plans to explore how she could have a new life in a place she loved.

Passionate about scuba diving, MJ began to explore how she could turn that hobby into a career. "Maybe I could work at a dive shop or take groups out on dives from a hotel or something," she suggested. She researched certification requirements and the financial commitment needed for such a life. She traded a good salary for a job at a dive shop in Missouri that would give her hands-on experience with equipment and teaching, preparing her for the same kind of work in Hawaii. Then she planned a three-week vacation to Kauai.

Prior to her scheduled return to the mainland, MJ called Ann. "Guess what? I'm not coming back! I have a job at a dive shop, I found a great apartment through a new friend at the church I've been visiting, and I think I can make it work here!" Ann shared MJ's news with the Goal Sisters, who were stunned at her "spontaneous" decision and impressed by her willingness to go after what she wanted.

And MJ did it. She forged a new life on Kauai, with friends, fun, and focused work time. She even had a Goal Sister meeting with Michelle on Oahu, including a hike, swimming, and, of course, time to talk about their goals. But then some homesickness kicked in: "I love it here, but I miss my house and my friends there! I wonder if I can have both."

Of course, the Goal Sisters told her that she could! Through the group's monthly meetings and some extra coaching with Ann, MJ is now designing a life that gives her four to five months in Hawaii, and the rest of the year in Missouri with her family, Goal Sisters, and other friends. She's creating a career that gives her the income to manage both places comfortably. MJ has journaled about her desired life, given thanks for her opportunities, and prayed hard for guidance to follow the divine direction she feels in her heart. She's living La Vida Goal Sister!

And how has MJ's progress influenced the other Goal Sisters? They have marveled at what MJ has accomplished and are grateful for being part of MJ's experience of seeing that anything is possible.

Sometimes you and your Goal Sister may be interested in doing major planting in the same kind of goal garden. You might be working at different paces, perhaps with one of you maintaining growth in your garden while the other is only starting to plant her goal seeds. We encourage you to share information about your experiences and be supportive of each other's individual planting efforts.

Ann and Michelle's Story

For many years, we both had health goals to become physically fit. At some point, we finally put our thoughts into action. Michelle went first. She didn't want to be fat at forty, so she enrolled in land-and-water aerobics classes at the Bloomington YWCA. Ann was living in Missouri at the time, so many of our discussions about our health goals took place via e-mail.

2/14/01
From: MBP
To: AL

So, I'm tired; just got back from aerobics. I was moving around like a slap-happy slug today, but I only clapped once out of sync with the group...three cheers for me!

Michelle continued to take aerobic classes five times a week and eat a low-fat, high-carbohydrate diet. She started to see results, and she shared her progress with Ann.

A year after Michelle first committed to working on her health goals, Ann ended a seven-year relationship with her significant other and started the exercise program outlined in the book Eight Minutes in the Morning. *Exercising helped her to cope and feel stronger. Ann noticed additional results within several months. She was inspired by how good she continued to feel, and by all the weight she was shedding. We continued to share our progress toward achieving our health goals.*

2/14/02
From: AL
To: MBP

I'm loving the aquasize class! Let's see, I'm doing that, walking every day, doing *Eight Minutes in the Morning*, playing tennis with Arlese once a week, and taking an African dance class. Almost sounds like I'm an active athletic type, huh?

Imagine how much it mattered to have someone out there encouraging our first steps and celebrating every step we took toward our fitness goals! Wait a second; you *know* how that feels because you have your own Goal Sister. Give thanks to her now for being there alongside you on your garden path to a great life.

Building a Community Garden

As you continue to work toward your goals, don't forget to keep your loved ones informed of your efforts. They may be curious about your exploration and what you're learning. They may want to know about your Goal Sister friendship and how it's benefiting you and them. They may need some encouragement from you. Feel free to dish out gratitude for the support your loved ones have given you. We also encourage you to talk about additional ways in which your loved ones can support you, now that you have a better idea of what's involved in working on your goals.

You have discovered the tools to use and the issues to pay attention to as you move forward with your goal setting and achievement efforts. But be aware that the pesky bugs who question your abilities aren't the only ones who might cause you to stumble on your garden path. In the next chapter, you'll see how you and your thoughts can become your own obstacle to success.

Chapter 6 Summary

★ You have a garden path, and your Goal Sister has her own path. Your commitment to your Goal Sister friendship means that you are willing to develop yourself and your garden while sharing your gardening wisdom with her, just as she's developing herself and her own garden.

★ Before you begin to plant your goal garden, build a garden shed that will motivate you toward success. This will be your primary place for thinking and planning.

★ Inventory your gardening gear and make sure you have good tools (a daily planner, computer, eyeglasses) to enhance your efforts toward your goals. Give yourself the necessary time, energy, and commitment (your "sunlight") to achieve your goals.

★ Make sure that your ideas and beliefs are tilled and ready for planting. Generate ways to compost your limiting beliefs so that they don't inhibit your goal flowers from blooming. Let your Goal Sister know when you want encouragement and support.

★ Work with your Goal Sister to assess your ability to grow more than a single variety of goals at this time. Your best initial option might be to start with your Small Goals, then progress to larger goals and other varieties in another season.

★ Keep your Goal Sister informed about your plans, your decision points, and the results of your efforts. Your efforts will inspire her to reach her goals, too! Let your loved ones know about your progress so that you can all enjoy the beauty of your blossoming goal flowers!

Questions

★ *What obstacle holds you back from planting your goal garden?*

★ *How can you prevent pesky bugs from eating away at your confidence as you move toward your goals?*

Chapter 7

When You and Your Thoughts Become Obstacles

Y ou're working toward your goals, and you're making progress! It's exciting — and maybe a little overwhelming. Don't worry, Goal Sister; it makes sense to feel a bit overwhelmed at this stage. We are rarely encouraged to think bigger and move beyond other people's expectations. It's not that our loved ones don't want the best for us; they do. But they count on us to be there for them in ways they've come to expect. Now that we're becoming who we want to be, we don't necessarily fit our loved ones' expectations — or even our own.

Let's face it: It's not just our loved ones who are unsure about our changes; we often feel the same tensions. We want to change parts of our lives, yet we don't want to change. It's like picking off daisy petals: I want to lose weight, I don't feel like going to the gym today; I want to have that conversation with my friend, I don't want to make waves; I want to change jobs, I don't want to lose my pension. After you've had some success in meeting your goals, you're bound to feel unsure of yourself as you push on. If you're feeling a little stressed, imagine how your old friends Fear and Doubt are doing right now.

FEAR: Hey, she really is serious about this change stuff!

DOUBT: Yeah, this is the farthest she's ever gotten with taking care of herself.

FEAR: We'd better swing into action before she gets any farther!

It's a good thing you know they're on their way; you have time to prepare your response. We're sending out an SOS on your behalf!

SOS: Strengthening Our Selves

You're having one of those days — maybe one of those weeks! It's as if you're in the eye of the storm. Your head is spinning and your body's getting tossed around in the whirlpool of stress. It seems like it's all you can do to stay on top of your responsibilities at home and at work. Never mind those new priority goals you're working on; they'll have to get in line behind all your obligations.

If you're experiencing these feelings, it may be time to batten down the hatches, Goal Sister, and strengthen yourself. Here's how you can do this:

- Increase your level of self-care. "Not again," you think. "You two are always harping on self-care!" We do it because we know how important it is — and that it's one of the first things to go when you're feeling stressed. It may seem impossible to take care of yourself right now, but this is exactly when you need it most. Whether you exercise, listen to music, soak in a tub, or go to a movie, do something that puts your emotional and physical health first at least once every day.

- Focus your thoughts. Looking at what must be done today — and what you can realistically do — will help you prioritize.

- Be thankful. When we get caught up in feeling overwhelmed, we often forget what we have to be thankful for. There's always something to express gratitude for: the sun rising, the loving touch of your partner, your friend's laughter, the smell of a favorite food. Reviewing your gratitude list every day is a great way to push the overwhelming times away.

- Feed your soul. Life becomes a big struggle when we are disconnected from experiences that give us comfort, peace of mind, and love. Finding ways to remember that we're all connected to something greater helps us feel less alone. How can you do this? You might pray by yourself or with others. Perhaps you enjoy getting out in nature, reading a spiritually uplifting book, chanting, attending religious services, or lighting a candle at dusk. No matter how you do it, feeding your soul spiritually can help you feel centered and peaceful within yourself until the outer storm subsides.

Exercise 7.1: It's Now or Later

It's time to prioritize, Goal Sister! What do you feel needs to be done *now?* Take some time to write down everything that you feel needs your attention at this moment. Go back through your list and circle those tasks that *must* be done. As you evaluate each task, ask yourself, "Does this have to be done today?" If not, flip to your favorite time-management system and plan which tasks you will complete by what dates. You'll feel better knowing that you've built time into your life for taking care of these items.

Exercise 7.2: Feeding Your Soul

Within the next eight hours, sit down with your journal and make a list of fifteen things you would like to do to feed your soul. Don't edit this list! It's so easy to say, "That costs too much" or "I don't have time." Just let your thoughts flow and see what develops.

Ann's Story

I have to admit that only in the past ten years have I shifted to truly taking care of myself. Working hard for my own business and other employers while managing all the rest of life's requirements took its toll. As I look back on it now, I see that rushing to do and be everything was really about not doing my grief work for all the losses I had experienced in my life.

My lesson has been to realize that if we don't allow ourselves to take time to acknowledge and care for our emotions (good and bad), our physical bodies will let us know something's wrong. I noticed that I had a distinct pattern of coming down with a cold or sore throat when I was at my most harried. I subconsciously knew that I needed to slow down, and my body faithfully did its part by becoming sick.

When I realized this, I started allowing myself to feel my emotions. I also increased my level of exercise and began to drink more water. I let up on my self-imposed pressure to fill every moment with activity. I began a regular practice of meditation and journaling. I remembered to breathe. And I gave up the notion of how I "should" look and feel, and began to accept the way I really am, especially when interacting with friends and family.

As a Goal Sister, I wish there were a ready-made, universal formula for taking care of oneself. We all see the same billboards and magazine ads: Eat better and prevent cancer or a heart attack! Exercise and reduce your risk of whatever could potentially kill you! Yet we reject the advice, certain that it won't happen to us. I now see the value of these messages, and I'm grateful that I began paying attention to them.

I know that you can take good care of yourself, too. And I trust that you will do so when your time is right. When you do, you'll feel more balance, more peace, and more clarity in your life.

Being Pulled in Many Directions

We applaud you, Goal Sister, for admitting it when the going gets rough and for not throwing in the towel on your goals. Don't give up! Instead, gather your strength and center yourself as you experience the tug-of-war between your life as it was before you started working toward your goals and your life now. As you tug one way to make room for new things and experiences in your life, you are pulled the other way by the reasons why you "can't do this" and "should have done that." Sound familiar? See if any of the following statements ring true for you:

- "I really want to cut back on my volunteer activities so that I can have more time to pursue my musical career, but my son's school is having its annual fundraiser and no one else is willing to be the chairperson. I can't do both, so I've decided to skip the auditions for the upcoming musical production and wait for the next opportunity."

- "I didn't make it to my rugby championship game this week because I forgot that I had promised to let my friend borrow my pickup truck to move his stuff out of his mom's house. I felt badly for him and I couldn't say "no" when he asked if I would stay and help."

- "I fully intended to tell my boss that I couldn't work over-time on my birthday, but she was desperate. So instead of celebrating with my Goal Sister and other friends, I stayed late at the office and skipped dinner."

Giggling and conspiring, you see Guilt and Doubt holding onto the other end of the rope, pulling you back to the life you led before becoming a Goal Sister. Together, they're scheming a sabo-tage that will surely ground your efforts and dash your actions toward success. As if that weren't enough, their cell phones are poised, ready to call up Fear and invite her to join them on their end of the rope.

The good news is that you can release your end of the rope and say a quick "so long" before they scurry off. "Yeah, right," you say sarcastically, "I've tried releasing them before, Ann and Michelle, and it didn't work." Ah yes, we nod knowingly. You've just given your negative feelings an open invitation to stay for awhile. You might as well throw them a party!

Exercise 7.3: The Whine and Cheese Party

You've cleaned and straightened every space in your home. You have arranged the food on pretty platters. The candles are lit and mellow music is playing. You're ready for your guests. Fear, Doubt, and Guilt arrive first. Pity and Shame are dropped off ten minutes later. Regrets and bitterness show up together, arm in arm. Failure is the last to pull into your driveway; her car broke down three times on the way. Your guests start to cluster around each other, chattering loudly as they devour their food and guzzle their drinks.

Listen to their conversations. You might hear Fear say, "I don't have enough money. How can I leave a high-paying job to pursue my dreams?" Regret perks up and responds, "If you stick with that logic, I'll have a big role to play later!" Meanwhile, Doubt is moaning, "What was I thinking when I incorporated? I need a degree in business to be a boutique owner!" Several of the guests snicker. "Besides," adds Guilt, "it's not acceptable for women in my situation to do this sort of thing."

When there's a break in the conversation, grab your journal and write down all the reasons that are holding you back from making more progress toward your goals. Think about your current list of priority goals and why you can't work on them right now.

When you feel certain that you've gotten all your reasons for not proceeding onto paper, put down your journal and take a deep breath. Now take another one. Notice how you feel. Sad? Frustrated? Disappointed? While we may be tempted to surrender our desires to Fear and Doubt, there's often an inner nudging that reveals itself, telling us that whatever we are feeling and experiencing is okay. It's okay to feel pulled in several directions. It's okay to feel unsure. It's okay to let fear and doubt visit. It's all connected to your commitment to achieving your goals and living the life you want.

After a while, you notice that your party guests have all left without saying good-bye. You read the note they've left: "You ran out of whine and cheese, so we're outta here — for now!" Oh well, it's not like they've used good manners before.

Identifying Limiting Beliefs

We encourage you to begin shifting any thoughts and beliefs you have that impede your progress toward your goals. You have probably developed beliefs that need to be identified and understood before you can release them. Whether these beliefs come from your parents, other important people, your culture, your community, or society, you've probably internalized them until they're your own.

Exercise 7.4: Whose Beliefs Are They, Anyway?

Take some time now to reflect on your accomplishments and disappointments, from childhood until today. What are your proudest moments? Who had faith in your abilities? Who else was there as you basked in your glory? Write your responses in your journal.

Now we'd like to know about the times when you were more embarrassed than you'd ever want to admit. What happened, and how did people around you respond? Write down your most embarrassing memories.

You're not alone in having experienced moments that continue to shape how you feel about yourself. Through our work with other women who are following the Goal Sister process, we've heard a number of stories about the limiting beliefs women have about themselves. We've distilled these into five major beliefs that may sound familiar to you.

"I Don't Deserve Good Things in My Life"

One issue that keeps many women from having the life of their dreams is a feeling that they don't deserve it. For many years, we've been socialized to put the needs of our children, partner, friends, coworkers, or parents ahead of our own. We've been told that taking care of ourselves is selfish and self-centered. Some of us have had a string of bad-luck episodes that taught us that nothing good lasts for long. If any of these experiences ring true for you, Goal Sister, they may have led you to develop a belief that you don't deserve a good life.

Michelle's Story

Ann's spiritual life has been a positive influence for me. Over the years, she's shown me how to walk one's spiritual talk, without preaching or pushing her views onto me or others. I didn't have spiritual goals when we first met as Goal Sisters; spirituality simply wasn't an active part of my life. It's hard to admit, but I didn't believe that I deserved spiritual goodness in my life because I hadn't thought about spirituality or practiced it for so many years. But Ann didn't judge me the way I judged myself, and she didn't make a big deal about it when I finally came up with my first spiritual goals after we'd been meeting for six years:

1. Meditate

2. Read books about mindfulness daily

Until then, I hadn't done either of these activities.

I decided to take a different spiritual path than Ann, who was part of a church community, attended services, and belonged to prayer groups. I was attracted to practicing Buddhism and mindfulness. My first action toward my spiritual goals was to visit a bookstore and skim every book on these topics. One of the first books I bought was Jon Kabat-Zinn's Wherever You Go, There You Are. *I read it section by section, and I tried many of the exercises. The sources listed in the back of the book led me to my next batch of books on mindfulness, which in turn led me to others.*

My next set of spiritual goals was:

1. Start each day reading a passage from one of my books on mindfulness and meditating on it.

2. Practice seeing Buddha in people around me.

3. Breathe.

4. Remember how it felt to be with my family and friends on our trip to Canada.

Ann was supportive of my new goals and gave me a book called What Would Buddha Do? *along with a bracelet inscribed with "WWBD." The bracelet proved very useful — both as a reminder to check my thoughts and actions against the Buddha's and as a conversation piece.*

Through the years, I've practiced mindfulness with my family, paid more attention to my breathing, and increased my level of trust in God. I've also incorporated these experiences into creating my artwork, which is leading me down another fulfilling path.

You do deserve all the good you can imagine — and then some — from sources you may not have considered. We believe this, and so do your Goal Sister and the people who love you.

"I'm Afraid of the Unknown"

If we're honest with ourselves, aren't we all a little afraid to do something we're unfamiliar with? For many of us, fear of the unknown is the most debilitating kind of fear. How can we possibly want something so much and yet have such doubts about it? How can we stay so miserable with ourselves and our situations when we know that the support and resources we need are available to us now? We sometimes forget that things worth having are worth stretching for. We may also forget that it's scary for everyone to take action toward something unfamiliar. People who rush into change and risk surely have doubts, yet they also see bigger possibilities; they trust themselves, and they trust the process.

Ann's Story

One big leap I took came after I'd been a Goal Sister for five years. I'm telling you about this leap because it shows that, no matter where we are in the Goal Sister process, our thoughts and feelings have power. I really needed — and received — the support of my Goal Sister to get me through this one.

I had been working as a life coach on a part-time basis for a couple of years, and I wanted to build my coaching into a full-time business. I also wanted to get back into giving workshops and doing more writing. In the past, I'd been successful in both areas, so I knew I could do it.

Meanwhile, I had a full-time job as a counselor and coach for at-risk teens. It was the second job I'd taken after moving from Illinois to Missouri. I enjoyed working with that age group, and I had great rapport with my clients; we did some good work together. The money was okay, the benefits were helpful, and the director was a dream to work for. I loved the job, but the hours restricted my creativity. I'm sure you can imagine what came next: the doubts!

DOUBTS: Why would I want to leave this security? Why would I give up the fun, sense of purpose, and rewards I'm receiving? Why would anyone in her right mind leave this great comfort zone to risk it all?

ME: I have to do this because I know I can have an even greater impact on other people's lives with my own work.

This tug-of-war went on for a while. As my spiritual guidance gained more solid footing, the pull toward leaving my job became stronger. I knew in my heart that it was the right thing to do, yet my fears were just as real.

FEARS: What if it doesn't work out? What if I never make any money? What if people didn't really want what I have to offer?

My fears and doubts washed over me in waves. I ago-nized over the decision for months. Many people around me didn't understand what I was going through. "Just do it, Ann!" they said, "What are you waiting for?" Still, I doubted.

Then three things happened to let me know that it was time. First, a good friend sent me a print by Brian Andreas. Brian's company, Story People, combines his art and words in whimsical drawings that reach one's gut and one's soul. This one was entitled "Waiting for Signs," and it included the line, "Then an angel in black tights came to me and said, 'You can start any time now.'" Second, Michelle said, "I think you should just leap and go for it," and sent me the Jane Evershed print entitled "The Leap of Faith." I started to see a theme! Third, my own personal coach, Nancy, challenged me by ask-ing, "If you claim to be such a spiritually in-tune person, how dare you not fulfill the role God has for you to play?"

So I did it! I made an appointment to talk with my boss about my needs and plans. Together, we explored an arrange-ment that would allow me to work part-time as I made the transition to having my own full-time coaching business. That felt good. I could still work with a group of people I loved and have some income to keep me stable until my business took off.

It was wonderful, intense, scary, and fulfilling. I would do it again in a minute. But next time, I would want to do it without the doubts and fears and the agonizing time it took to make the decision. I know, however, that life doesn't work that way. We need the energy of our doubts and fears to really move us forward — no matter how much support we have, no matter how sure we are. The bottom line is that we need to trust the process, trust our intentions, and stay true to our vision. I am so glad I took the leap!

We've both felt the butterflies in our stomachs, experienced the sweaty palms and tightness in our chests, and dealt with the lumps in our throats that indicated we were onto something big. Each leap we take seems to let us know that we don't need to go back to our old fears of the unknown.

"Something Bad Will Come from Change"

Are you a "what if" worrier? Are you the one among your friends who, no matter what great idea or good news is presented, says, "Yes, but what if it doesn't work? What if the money isn't there? What if something goes wrong? What if I make a mistake? What if, what if, what if?" If you're that kind of "what if" person, you're not alone. Indeed, many people would say that it's good common sense to be cautious and to plan well for the future. We agree. Yet you might be reverting to old, familiar ways because you're afraid of change. Let's take this limiting belief out for a new-perspective spin.

Exercise 7.5: For Your Own Good

Think about some things you've been criticized for during the last year. For example, you may have been criticized for always being late to functions, for being a workaholic, or for the way you live. Take out your journal and write down five criticisms you've received.

Now take a page for each criticism and write the positive version of it at the top of the page after the words "25 Wonderful Things That Might Happen to Me If I. . . ." For example, if the criticism is "I've been criticized for not caring about my looks," you would write: "25 Wonderful Things That Might Happen to Me If I Cared about My Looks." Do this for all five criticisms. Talk with your Goal Sister about your fear of change and about what you learned from this exercise.

"It's Not My Time"

We've all heard about the discussion between two people, in which one expresses her desire to return to college despite her "old age." But she fears that her time has passed and she's too old to accomplish what her heart desires. "How old are you?" asks her friend. "I am forty-five," she responds, "and by the time I get through school I'll be forty-nine." Her friend asks, "And how old will you be in four years if you don't go to school?"

Dear Goal Sister, if this book does nothing else for you, please let it motivate you to try — to take a step toward an even greater life for yourself, to taste the possibility of what is ahead for you.

Michelle's Story

When Ann and I began receiving encouraging feedback about writing this book, I became full of doubts about whether it was the right time to start a new career as a writer. Why would I put my relationships at stake when our family had just moved and our lives were still in flux? Why would I change careers when there wasn't any guarantee that Goal Sisters *would be successful? Why would I commit time and money that could otherwise be devoted to other people and other areas of my life? Why would I want to do all this* now?

I obsessed about this decision, and initially I let my self-doubts run amok. My doubts convinced me that if I pursued writing this book now, I would end up emotionally and financially broke, Bart would feel abandoned and dumped on, and Zoë and Kanoa would grow up hating and not knowing me. Luckily, a louder voice inside of me said, "If not now, when?" It was the same voice I'd once heard when Bart and I were talking about having a baby. Back then, there were so many reasons why it wasn't the right time to start our family. Yet we felt compelled to do so; we loved each other, we knew we'd be great parents, and we wanted to have children while we were young. Hearing that voice again reminded me that there isn't a perfect time to make big changes in your life, and that sometimes you have to trust your gut and go for it.

Another voice convinced me to act now instead of later: the enthusiasm, confidence, and buoyancy of my own voice when I talked about Goal Sisters. *Everyone noticed how pumped up I got! I heard the same excitement in Ann's voice. I received so much support from Bart to take this step now that the voice of my self-doubts eventually faded into the background.*

Once I chose to move ahead with this book, I didn't second-guess my decision, and neither did my family. They inspire me daily to create the best book I can. In return, I hope that my actions inspire them to believe in themselves, trust their inner voice, and have faith in their ability to know when the time is right for taking action.

"I'll Lose the Comfortable Lifestyle I Have Now"

What if you could maintain, or even increase, the level of comfort, contentment, and financial success you have now by doing what you truly want to do? Wouldn't your friends and family encourage you to take the steps that would make you truly happy, even if that means sacrificing in the short run? Wouldn't your loved ones ultimately benefit from seeing you meet life head-on, with passion, excitement, and confidence? We believe that they would admire your courage and think of you as someone who went after her dreams — who took carefully thought-out risks and learned new things about herself. We believe this because we've seen it happen in our lives and with our friends.

Michelle's Story

My friend Liz was imprisoned by the fear of losing her comfortable lifestyle. She wanted to leave a career that paid well and made a big difference in people's lives. The problem was, her job didn't nourish her creative side. Liz had been an opera singer years before, and she wanted to live that life again. Her partner didn't work regularly and contributed much less to their family income. So the stakes were high: If she quit, they'd lose their health insurance, they couldn't afford to travel much, and their children would go without. "Without what?" I asked. "Without the bad moods you've been in because you're so stressed out?"

She got it. After mulling it over and talking with her partner, Liz started taking steps to leave her job. She told her boss about her plans, and they designed a way to decrease her work hours. Her company recognized how much Liz had contributed, and they arranged for her to continue receiving insurance benefits for six months after she left. She was thrilled! She informed all the people who reported to her about her desires, and most of them supported her in her quest. As Liz decreased her hours at work, she started going after new creative opportunities. She also started spending more time with her children during the day.

Liz's transition didn't take her straight from point A to point B. She actually took on other noncreative jobs to provide income while she left the job she no longer wanted. This showed Liz, among other things, that she was capable of finding other work, that she could juggle different jobs, and that people wanted to hire her.

Today, Liz's work life is equally divided between creative and noncreative jobs. After giving herself permission to leave her full-time job and take on consulting gigs, she realized that she hadn't lost her interest in the work itself; it was just that she wanted more freedom to take on new activities. Liz still worries about health insurance and how her family will maintain their lifestyle, but now her worries set her into action.

Like Liz, you may be allowing the practical details of daily living to stand in the way of making big life changes. Having a heightened awareness of what you want to move toward is a great start in dealing with those beliefs. Amazingly, once you know what you want, the events and people in your life will begin to give you signals that it's time to move into action to accomplish your goals. Your readiness for a change might start as a slight feeling of discontentment with your present situation, or you might notice that you're easily irritated by life's little happenings. Or maybe you're experiencing a feeling of emptiness that wasn't there before. We encourage you to be aware of your feelings and to create new beliefs that your faith in your desire is bigger than your fears.

Reframing Your Limiting Beliefs

Now that we've listed the top five limiting beliefs we encounter among women, here's a news flash: You can change how you relate to your old limiting beliefs. Work through the following exercises to begin the process of seeing your fears and doubts from a new perspective and changing your limiting beliefs into beliefs that serve you and your desires now.

Exercise 7.6: Thank-You Notes

It's been a while since you held your whine and cheese party. You have some free time this afternoon, so you decide to write thank-you notes to your guests. Take some time to think about all the ways in which your fears and doubts have helped you in the past. How have they protected you from failing at something? How have they looked after your best interests?

For example, let's say that you and your roommate are in the process of buying a franchise business. You've been excited about this partnership and you're ecstatic that your roommate arranged an appointment with some potential financial backers for next week. You both need to put together a knockout business plan and presentation. As you sit down to write your part of the plan, you begin to doubt whether the two of you can pull this off. You feel the pressure build inside you. It's your first business venture, and you don't want to fail. Your fears and doubts know that a partial commitment to a new partnership might translate into a mediocre business plan and a less-than-enthusiastic attitude at your upcoming meeting. Your fears and doubts are trying to save you from losing face and having those negative experiences by putting the brakes on your efforts now. Isn't that a wonderful gift? No wonder they've been your friends for a while. Difficult as it may be to see it this way, your limiting beliefs have been gifts from your fears and doubts; they deserve to be thanked.

Take out your journal and fill in this thank-you note to each of your fears and doubts:

Dear _____,

Thank you for protecting me all these years from feeling _____ and _____. I especially appreciate how you _____. It would have been difficult for me to face some of those feelings and take some of those risks back then, but I'm ready to do that now and I'm ready to let go of your gifts. You see, I don't need your help anymore. I'm ready to have a stronger friendship with Confidence, Trust, and Clarity. With them and my Goal Sister, I will continue to achieve my goals and become who I want to be.

Best wishes,
[You]

How did it feel to write those notes in your journal? Strange? Exhilarating? Fun? How do you feel about letting your fears and doubts go so that you can proceed toward your goals? Confident? Hopeful? Write down your responses and feelings and share them later with your Goal Sister.

Exercise 7.7: To Believe or Not to Believe?

Revisit the notes you made during your whine and cheese party and look at the list of reasons why you can't have your great life. These reasons are based in old, limiting beliefs. Take a few minutes to list them on a new page of your journal.

How do you know if a given belief is healthy or unhealthy for you? In his workshops, noted author Dr. O. Carl Simonton suggests that you ask yourself five questions about each of your beliefs:

1. Is it a fact?

2. Does this belief support my life and health?

3. Does it support my long- and short-term growth?

4. Does it help me avoid undesirable conflict?

5. Does it help me feel the way I want to feel?

If you answer "yes" to three of these five questions, then your belief is probably a healthy one.

Now go back and consider each belief. Next to it, record a positive belief or statement. For example:

Negative Belief	Positive Belief
"I need a degree to succeed."	"I have more than enough talent to meet my goals."

Next, write your positive beliefs on an index card and carry the card with you. Three times a day, quiet your mind and read through your positive beliefs. Allow yourself to see them becoming your truth. Look at your calendar and count ahead six weeks. On that date, take some time to reflect on and reevaluate your level of faith in your new beliefs. Congratulate yourself for this new habit!

After you've been affirming your new positive beliefs three times a day for twenty-one days, it's time to anchor them in for the long term. An action step might be to display pictures of an event similar to what you want to do. Or you might update your résumé. Brainstorm actions for each of your positive beliefs. This does take work and energy, Goal Sister. This exercise will stretch your mind muscles and bring you great rewards.

~~~~~~~~~~~

There is a spiritual principle that says: "Thoughts held in mind produce after their kind." Think thoughts that affirm the possibilities within your reach. Replace your limiting beliefs with healthy beliefs that support you in reaching your goals. Activate and practice your healthy beliefs as you take your own leap of faith, in thought and action, toward increased happiness and success.

Chapter 7 Summary

★ Juggling your new goal-achievement actions with existing demands on your time and attention may cause you to feel overwhelmed. That's to be expected! You can temper your stress by increasing your self-care, focusing your thoughts and energy, showing gratitude, and feeding your soul.

★ Your continued progress toward your goals might be impeded by your limiting beliefs. If that's so, take time to reflect on where these beliefs originated and what purpose they serve in your life.

★ Which of these limiting beliefs sound familiar?

- "I don't deserve good things in my life."
- "I'm afraid of the unknown."
- "Something bad will come from change."
- "It's not my time."
- "I'll lose the comfortable lifestyle I have now."

★ Naming your limiting beliefs will help you to identify where you're struggling. Reframe those limiting beliefs and use them to your advantage.

Questions

★ *How do you plan to feed your soul this week?*

★ *What new experience might you have if you reframe your limiting beliefs?*

Chapter 8

Calling All Goal Sisters Seeking Support and Sanity!

Let's say you've spent all morning talking to your e-mail provider and your computer company as part of meeting your "figure out why my e-mail isn't working" goal. You're just getting off the phone with the fourth technician you've talked to after he tells you, "I'm sorry, but that's not under our company's jurisdiction; you'll have to call such-and-such company for the help you need." Right about now, you want to throw your computer out the window — where it will land on top of your telephone! But you decide not to do that. Instead, you take a breath and make one more phone call. Who you gonna call? Your Goal Sister! She'll listen as you vent. She'll commiserate with you. She'll give you additional ideas for solving this conundrum, if that's what you ask for. And as her Goal Sister, you won't just dump your troubles on her and run; you'll allow her equal time to bend your ear as well. Remember: Yours is a give-and-take friendship, and that goes both ways!

Like a beautiful diamond, there are many facets to your Goal Sister friendship. Whether it's the way you're there for each other in moments of need, the way you help each other problem-solve when you're stuck, the way you give each other permission to do what needs to be done, or the way you keep each other account-able, your Goal Sister friendship boldly goes where other friend-ships leave off. It sparkles brightly as the two of you progress in your relationship and toward your goals.

Just Call Out Her Name

As a Goal Sister, the quality of your presence and attention sets this relationship apart from your other friendships. The following traits are essential features of your Goal Sister friendship:

Active Listening

No matter which of you has sent out a call for help, the best response you can give each other is to practice the art of active lis-tening. Focus totally on your Goal Sister and her needs in your conversation. Be present in each moment. We've all had the expe-rience of knowing when someone is not really listening to us. It may not be personal; she may have a full plate and be thinking ahead to the tasks she still needs to complete by the end of the day. Ask your Goal Sister for her full attention if that's what you need. If she can't give it to you, she'll be honest and tell you so, in which case you can schedule another time to talk.

Asking Her What She Needs

Whether it's the end of a Goal Sister meeting or your Goal Sis-ter has just contacted you for help, ask her, "How do you want me to help you?" This gives her a chance to tell you how she'd like to be supported or held accountable. For example, she might say, "I need you to call me every morning at 7:00 A.M. to make sure I write my two pages." Or she might say, "I'd really appre-ciate it if you could go to the doctor with me when I get my test results."

Michelle's Story

After Ann moved to Missouri in 1997, Faith and I continued to meet as Goal Sisters in person every quarter. Our conversations mostly focused on our consulting businesses and our business goals. We had fun sharing information and resources. Faith passed on information about the school district, which I used to write a grant proposal. She also filled me in on the history of conflict between the two school districts where we lived. I showed Faith how to work with Excel spreadsheets, and I gave her some focus-group materials. We didn't really ask or need much from each other, which was good for us because our lives were pretty full.

In January of 1998, Faith and I drove down to St. Louis for an overnight meeting with Ann. We had a fun, productive twenty-four hours of shopping, goal setting, problem solving, eating out, and action planning. On the way back from St. Louis, Faith and I spent some time talking about our next quarter's business goals, but we mostly shared concerns we had about various family issues. We appreciated each other's perspectives and were grateful that we could talk at length about other topics of interest.

Whether you're talking about your goals or connecting in other ways, it's important to find out what you need from your friendship and to be open to sharing.

Accepting Her "As Is"

At some point in your friendship, you may feel compelled to call your Goal Sister on her thoughts and actions. Be careful, though, that your comments aren't laced with criticism and judgment. For example, your Goal Sister may tell you for the hundredth time that she's tired of being mistreated by a certain friend and wants to end their friendship. From your perspective, she hasn't made any noticeable steps toward doing so. It might be tempting to say, "Why can't you just tell her how you feel and be done with it? All you do is complain about this person. Complain, complain, complain. When are you going to figure out that you need to stop hanging out with her?" Whoa, Goal Sister! It's okay for you to have these thoughts, but it's not okay for you to express them as criticism and judgment. An alternative response might be: "You know, you've been talking about how unhappy you are with this friendship for a long time. Is this an area you want to work on and set some goals for?" While it may be frustrating to not speak your entire truth about a situation, in the Goal Sister process it's essential to respect each other's paths. Your Goal Sister has her path; you have yours. If she asks for your opinion, tell her what you think in a nonjudgmental way. Gently point out how her thinking and actions don't match her stated goals and intentions. Remind her that actions speak louder than words. Here's an example of how to accomplish that:

9/16/01
From: AL
To: MBP

My priority goal list is coming along...I will have it to you by the end of the day. Regarding yours, perhaps because it is really MY issue, I sense more inaction in your goals. Reading and doing thought-provoking exercises is good, but when will you DO it for YOU? You know how we always talk about me planning, planning, planning until the cows come home...I just started to feel that same quality in your writings. Food for thought; maybe it's nothing, but I thought I would mention it.

Appreciating Her

Show your Goal Sister gratitude for being there. When we feel stuck or we're in crisis mode, it's good to know that we appreciate each other's support and don't take each other's listening ear and heart for granted. Letting your Goal Sister know that you're thankful for her confidence and her stick-to-itiveness around a tough goal is also a great way to show your appreciation. The following e-mail demonstrates Michelle's response to learning that Ann's just lost another ten pounds as part of her new healthy lifestyle:

7/19/02
From: MBP
To: AL

Speaking of real living, I'm so glad to hear that you've released so much of your weight and unhealthy habits, and that you can feel things more intensely than you did before. Whether it's happiness, sadness, joy, fear, ecstasy, loneliness — you're feeling things more, and I see you continuing to do so. You really are a brave soul, my friend, and I admire you for not taking the easy, familiar, well-worn path. You're creating a dazzling new path! It may have a lot of unpredictable twists and turns, but hey — would you really want it any other way? Okay, maybe some days you would. That's where the balance comes in — something we both need to continue incorporating into our lives.

Telling your Goal Sister that you appreciate her strengths and that you celebrate her "walking her talk" can be uplifting and energizing for both of you.

Two Heads Are Better than One: Problem Solving Together

When you get frustrated or hit a wall in working toward your goals, don't hesitate to ask your Goal Sister for help with problem solving. When you do, ask for specific kinds of help, such as: "I need help figuring out how to include more exercise in my day," or "Can you help me decide how to say 'no' to things I don't want to do?" Your Goal Sister will have a more objective view of the problem, which will give you more options to explore. Give her a chance to consider the problem if she requests that, then schedule a time to talk about it with her later.

She's Not Just Another Damsel in Distress

While it's expected that you and your Goal Sister will be there to support each other, it's not okay to rescue each other from your challenges. For example, if one of you is experiencing ongoing difficulties with a significant other, it's not okay to use your Goal Sister as a sounding board after every disagreement or during every moment of despair over this relationship. On the receiving end, it's not okay as a Goal Sister to encourage that kind of dependence and support. It's just not healthy for your friendship.

Goal Sisters empower each other to make the right choices, but they don't try to save each other from making the wrong ones. When either of you is enduring tough challenges, it's important to stay within your Goal Sister friendship bounds by:

• Reminding yourselves that you're each on your own path

• Increasing your awareness of the words you use with each other

• Focusing on the Three E's:

   1. Encourage her to follow her path,

   2. Evaluate her options with her, and

   3. Enthusiastically support her newly defined action steps.

These actions will go a long way toward maintaining the integrity of your Goal Sister friendship, while empowering you to each overcome obstacles and move on to success.

Goal Sister Group Story

We all have good and bad days. The Goal Sister Group members cope with these highs and lows in their regular meetings. Most of the meetings happen at Ann's home, where she has a comfy, oversized recliner nestled beside the couch and the end table.

You know the expression "If these walls could talk…"? That's how the group members feel about that recliner! It seems to attract the woman who has the greatest need to release her emotions. Each group member who happens to sit in it has shared not only her successes in goal achievement, but also her current frustrations with life's ups and downs. That often means tears. They've sobbed about family challenges, relationship obstacles, and insensitive coworkers. They've cried for lives not fully lived, hopes that were dashed, and desires that were shelved years ago.

No matter who ends up crying in the recliner, the other Goal Sisters rally around and do what they do best: accept their Sister's feelings and support her in finding her next step. With just the right balance of active listening and encouragement, they tackle the challenge head on. Whether they suggest a new way of looking at the problem or devise a small, specific action to take, the Goal Sisters leave the meeting with a little more confidence and a lot more hope.

Develop New Ways to Respond to Old Stressors

We all fall into emotional holes from time to time: holes of past mistakes and holes of past behaviors we'd like to forget. Sometimes our holes are our limiting beliefs, other times they are our responses to stress. Falling into an emotional hole usually leads to a familiar place that's not productive for you.

Michelle's Story

I was a stressed-out wild woman two weeks before Bart and I put our home of ten years up for sale. There were so many things to go through and pack or give away, so many things to clean, so many walls to paint. It would have been easy to succumb to the stress I felt and make my family's life an emotional hell.

But I chose not to do that. Instead, one morning I sat with my feelings of stress, took lots of deep breaths, and attempted to quiet my racing thoughts. I reminded myself that one of my strengths is creativity. "Okay, Michelle," I said to myself, "how can you creatively respond to your stress?" I sat for a while longer, giving myself permission to see where the stress was really coming from. The answer, along with my tears, didn't take long to arrive: My head knew that I had to get our home ready for sale, but my heart wasn't ready to say good-bye. Whatever I did during the next week, I knew then that I needed to come up with an imaginative way to say good-bye along the way. Later that week, I e-mailed Ann:

4/8/02
From: MBP
To: AL

Well, I've just finished packing about half my clothes from two closets, and I'm putting another bag of my clothes together for Goodwill. I've changed my attitude toward getting the house ready from griping and stressing out to "thanks for the memories" and "I'm doing my best to make sure we leave you looking your best!" So instead of cussing at all the clothes I have to go through, I take each one, look it over, and either fold it up neatly or thank it for keeping me warm/making me look stylish/the fun I had wearing it and place in the Goodwill bag. I'm not getting through my stuff very quickly, but it's much, much, much more enjoyable this way.

4/9/02
From: AL
To: MBP

I love this new attitude! Remember, it is all about gratitude and love. That's really all we have to focus on. And won't having that feeling in the house be much more attractive to the new buyer who comes through than the feelings of stress, anger, and resentment? You bet! The house will be sold by next Tuesday!

Guess what? Our house sold on the day Ann predicted, saving me from stressing out about keeping our home clean indefinitely. Changing my response to stress really worked!

We all fall into the same old emotional holes until we figure out that we don't have to fall into them anymore and do something different. It's incredibly freeing to fall a little way into a hole, recognize what's happening, lift ourselves out, then walk around the hole. Getting to that point requires that we make ongoing, deliberate choices to not fall in and get stuck anymore.

Having a Goal Sister to prompt and support you as you navigate your emotional holes makes a huge difference. We've developed a game to help each other recognize when we're falling into an emotional hole and responding in unproductive ways. We call our old, unproductive selves the "old Ann" and "old Michelle," and we say things like, "That thinking was so last decade, Ann" or "The old Michelle would have done nothing, but thank goodness the new Michelle goes into action."

Exercise 8.1: All Stressed Out, Nowhere to Go

Imagine that you're stressed beyond belief and you want to share the reasons with your Goal Sister. You're ready to get her help in gently moving forward on your path. Take a few minutes now to write down how you would like her to help you. Use a page in your journal to imagine her response to you in a way that would mean the most to you. Will she say, "I'll be right there! Do you want me to bring strawberry or triple-fudge ice cream?" Maybe she'll be a needed taskmaster and tell you that you have five minutes to complain, then you'll spend the next five minutes working together on a solution. We don't know how you would like her to help you, but you do. Write down your ideas and share them with your Goal Sister so that she will be prepared to support you when your stressed-out times occur.

Ann's Story

I love the spiritual home I've found in Unity Church. This nondenominational, Christian-based movement has served me well for over twenty years. Through my mother's death, career changes, and relationship changes, it was Unity that taught me that God's plan for me is greater than anything I can imagine for myself. How exciting and encouraging! How fulfilling it was to find a group of like-minded people who believe in God's abundance for our lives — and who will do the work to receive it! With a life like that, I wanted to give back in some way.

In addition to regular tithing, I decided to give my time and talents to Unity. One of the ways I did this was to serve on the board of trustees for both the church in Bloomington, Illinois, and the one in Joplin, Missouri. I felt that guiding the growth of the church was a great way to share all that I had received from the experience.

I served as president at the Joplin church, but at some point I determined that I was not willing to run for another term. There was one woman on the board who I thought would be the right successor, and I broached the subject with her. With great honesty, she confided in me that her heart was not in it; in fact, she was thinking of resigning from the board. She was tired of being one of the few people who did the work, without seeing much result in church growth. She then asked,

"Is that the kind of attitude you want in your president?" I assured her that it wasn't, and that she needed to follow her heart; if she couldn't give 100 percent, she should resign.

That conversation led me to consider my own commitment to serving the church in that way. I was tired, too. I was at a crucial point in building my business and I needed to spend more time and energy on it. I didn't want to feel that I had to be at every church meeting and function and that I had to be the one to find help for coping with emergencies like failing furnaces, clutter, and financial decisions. I had an "aha moment" when I realized that I couldn't give 100 percent myself, and that I needed to walk my talk. I too decided to resign from the board. I found other ways to serve the church that gave me a better sense of balance with my time and energy. It felt good to honor my own heart instead of just encouraging others to follow theirs.

I shared this decision with my Goal Sister. She had watched me struggle with these issues and demands, and was relieved to learn of my choice. She responded with the following e-mail:

10/17/01
From: MBP
To: AL

Let go of that old self of yours — that is, after honoring her and thanking her for getting you this far in your journey. Then make space for the new Ann — the one who sees the bumps in the day as bumps in the day. Make space for the focused Ann — the one who's going to come back from lunch and get back to her intentions. The "no longer a caregiver/rescuer/doormat" Ann who will no longer change everything in her day to let someone else take, take, take, take her support, caring, and nurturing. Welcome the businesswoman Ann, who's creating more information and services that will be bought by paying others in the Universe. I think you get it: See ya, old Ann, HELLO NEW ANN!

Affirming your Goal Sister's actions with your understanding and support can go a long way toward boosting her self-confidence and self-assurance.

Sort Out Your Feelings

Sorting out your feelings is especially important when your old limiting beliefs come to call. Helping your Goal Sister identify her feelings, then looking together at new ways to respond to them is a wonderful gift you can give each other.

Sister, Get Thee to a Therapist!

Your Goal Sister friendship is not meant to replace a relationship with a therapist. Some of us need additional help to sort through our feelings and keep from falling into emotional holes. If you or your Goal Sister feel like you need more help to cope with your feelings and your circumstances, we encourage you to contact a mental health professional and get the help you need and deserve.

Use Humor

You've heard the saying "If I don't laugh, I'll cry"? Laughter is healing and freeing. Laughter encourages us to lighten up on ourselves and our situation. Whether you head to a funny movie, spend time being silly with children, or laugh at yourself, give humor a place in your life. Using humor with your Goal Sister brings fun into talking about everyday responsibilities.

Michelle's Story

I constantly struggle with balancing being a researcher and being a wife and a mom. Over the years, I've learned to accept the tension among these roles as a given, and I understand that some days will be more balanced than others. My ongoing goal is to keep my career as a priority, but not to let it stay my number-one priority for too long. This isn't always easy, since my research work is cyclic; there are times when I have very little on my plate, and times when it's heaped with tasks to complete.

Sometimes I use humor to deal with this tension by referring to my research work as my "diner job." So instead of my Senior Research Associate title, I call myself a Senior Waitress. My "customers" are the eight study sites I work with. Here's an Instant Message conversation I had with Ann about my work:

MBP: Well, my dear, my St. Louis customers are yanking on my skirt again. Have to serve them their pie and coffee before the diner closes.

AL: Why don't you just send the customers to Denny's?

MBP: Because Denny's doesn't have our great selection of pies!

AL: That's true. Maybe the manager can see that you get a break?

MBP: Nope, not today. It's standing-room only; everyone wants a slice of pie! And the Seattle customers want lattés with their pie.

AL: Oh my! Okay, I'll meet you back here after your shift is over.

Referring to my research job as my diner job keeps me from getting bogged down in the tedious, unexciting parts of my work — and it gives Ann and me a chance to have some fun interactions.

Exercise 8.2: Lighten Up!

Take a few minutes to think about the role of humor in your life. What's the funniest movie you've ever seen? What is the funniest thing one of your kids has done? What time of your life was the most carefree, and why? What was the best practical joke you ever played on someone? When was the last time you got a bad case of the giggles? As you reflect on these memories, consider the last time you really laughed this past week. Do you need more laughter in your life?

Draw something funny and inspirational on a card for your Goal Sister. Call her or another friend and set a date to rent a funny movie and chuckle together. You'll both enjoy the chance to lighten up in a fun way.

You've Got My Permission

Isn't it funny how easily we give other people permission to go for what they want — while we don't always do the same for ourselves? Have you noticed how effortlessly we say, "I know you can do it!" to others, but not to ourselves? Actually, it isn't funny at all. Many of us have internalized our limiting beliefs to the point where we put ourselves down when we're not achieving our goals as quickly as we think we should. We sometimes say cruel things to ourselves, like "I'm just not smart enough" or "As usual, I blew it" or "I knew I couldn't do it."

Through the Goal Sister process, you are no doubt seeing proof that, even though you may be your own worst enemy, you and your Goal Sister are allies in finding ways to allow you to have a great life. Until you can do it for yourself, your Goal Sister will give you permission to stay stuck if you need to, to ask for help, to stop beating yourself up, and to readjust your expectations.

To Stay Stuck

"I give you permission to make mistakes and stay stuck in them!" your Goal Sister declares. "How strange," you muse. Yet we know that nothing is coincidental, right? There is, no doubt, a valuable lesson for all of us in making mistakes. How else would we really learn so that we'll make a different choice next time? Your Goal Sister will let you wallow in your stuckness until you get the lesson you're supposed to get and hightail it out of the muck.

To Ask for Help from Other Supportive People

Your Goal Sister understands that answers come from both expected and unexpected sources. She'll encourage you to check out all of your resources and to make requests for what you need to get you through the crunch times. It's tough to ask for help, we know. When we're stressed out, most of us feel like we have to take care of everything ALL BY OURSELVES. Your Goal Sister will give you permission to ask for help by encouraging you to look at your list of things to do and dole out some of your obligations.

Together, you can problem-solve, brainstorming on the following questions:

- Is there something your partner can help you out with?
- Can your kids do some of the chores?
- Can a friend help with some of your errands?
- Can you take back your offer to volunteer this week?

You'll feel a lot better if you share some of your to-do list with those you love. And they'll be happy to help you, knowing they're relieving you of some of your stress.

To Stop Beating Yourself Up

Who else but your Goal Sister will tell you firmly and kindly to stop beating yourself up? She'll encourage you to give yourself a break and stay emotionally afloat until the storm in your life subsides. She'll help you see that no good comes from beating yourself up for past or current mistakes and shortcomings. She'll help you understand that self-abusive thoughts only serve to keep you

in a negative place of doubt and misery. Here's an e-mail example
of how we helped each other stop the self-flagellation:

4/24/02
From: AL
To: MBP

I'm sorry, but I'm just not going to be able to send the chapter draft
today. I'm going to have to focus my energy on getting articles completed. I'm having trouble getting to Websites for additional information
that I need, so that means I'm going to need to contact people again
and that all takes TIME! Yes, I'm overwhelmed today! I want to do our
invitation. I want to do our proposal. I want to exercise more. I want to
make some money. I want a lot of stuff, but right now I have to get this
magazine stuff done. I'm sorry I'm such a failure as a Goal Sister!

4/24/02
From: MBP
To: AL

Okay, so now that you've beaten yourself up and you've stated that
you want to do a lot of things you're currently not doing, what's
going to help you continue releasing the OLD, taking in the NEW,
and balancing it all? What do you need to do differently NOW?
Take a breath first, my friend, and see what you come up with.

4/25/02
From: AL
To: MBP

I just want to thank you for being such a terrific Goal Sister by keeping on talking to me about the benefits of exercising when I get stressed
out. I feel great! I did my exercises this morning and took a long walk.
It really cleared my head. You always hear that walking will do that,
and today I got to that point where my edginess faded. It feels so good!

Until you stop beating yourself up, count on your Goal Sister
to call you on your stuff.

Exercise 8.3: Beat The Drum Lightly

Take out your journal and time yourself for five minutes as you complete this sentence: "I hate it when I _____." Don't edit your thoughts. Don't worry about punctuation or grammar. Just let your hand write for five minutes about the things you hate. If you find that your mind goes blank, start again with the same phrase: "I hate it when I _____" and fill in whatever comes to mind. Just let it flow.

Did you notice how beating yourself up on one thing often dominoes into beating yourself up on another? "I'm so mad at myself for not sewing that jacket" starts blurring into "I hate how I look in these jeans" to "I'm such a lousy partner" to "I can't do anything right." STOP IT! If this sounds all too familiar, call your Goal Sister immediately and create a goal to work on your domino thoughts.

To Readjust Your Goals and Expectations

Your Goal Sister will let you know that it's okay to take smaller steps than you originally expected to take. She'll tell you that it's okay to think big, and that it's okay to ease up on yourself if you don't achieve a goal as you expected. She'll encourage you to bend your expectations — something many of us have forgotten how to do as adults.

Michelle's Story

I'll leave it to the wisdom of a child to illustrate this point. My eleven-year-old son, Kanoa, likes to play a particular game whenever he puts away a dishwasher-load of dishes. Kanoa puts on a CD of Israel Kamakawiwo'ole's songs, then starts the song "Somewhere Over the Rainbow/What a Wonderful World." He challenges himself to finish unloading the dishwasher before the song ends. One night, when Bart and I were fixing dinner and making it hard for Kanoa to get to key drawers and cabinets, he was unable to finish before the song was over. Instead of getting down on himself, Kanoa said, "Oh well, I might not have done it by the end of the song, but I'm going to put them all away before the end of the CD!" Then he went on his merry way and completed his task.

Not only do you have permission from your Goal Sister to be who you are, lighten up on yourself and live out your desires, but you can give yourself that same permission. The world won't end. The sky won't fall. In fact, you'll probably end up feeling happier and healthier.

Are You My Codependent Goal Sister?

If you feel like contacting your Goal Sister about every little change you make or every obstacle you encounter, don't! You're not hooked up to her intravenously! When you need support, ask for it. When you feel she needs contact, offer it. As Goal Sisters, we empower and draw strength from one another, not blood. That means being respectful of how your Goal Sister can help you while not taking advantage of her time and kindness. That means using her strengths to complement yours and not overstepping your Goal Sister friendship bounds. How will you know if you've gone too far? Ask her! She'll let you know, because this friendship is as important to her as it is to you.

Giving and Receiving Encouragement

Supporting and motivating your Goal Sister is the foundation of this process. We're at our best when we take the time to encourage each other to make the first, second, or hundredth step toward achieving our goals. Whether you say "way to go," send her a card, or cheer her on, it will mean a lot to your Goal Sister.

Why is encouragement so important? Giving and receiving love, acceptance, and encouragement can move us forward to a better life. You've been alone and uncomfortable before, but you're not alone any more. Somewhere out there is your Goal Sister, and she knows what you're worried about, what your intentions are, and what your strengths are. She's there with you in spirit, if not just a phone call away. The following Instant Message exchange is a good example of how we've encouraged each other.

AL: What would you say if I told you I don't want to mess with the business expo next week? I really am feeling that people go to that only to get free stuff and throw away whatever else they pick up. I think I could reach my target audience a lot better doing other things...
MBP: I would say that's a great decision! I would say you're getting smarter about where you can find real clients. I would say you're brilliant!

When the stress of life gets you down, take heart. You can get back on track, and your Goal Sister will do her best to show you how. When things get tough, it's time to refocus and put your mind on your goals. We believe that you can harness your thoughts and get back on your path to success. To help ease yourself back on track, try the following suggestions:

Flex Your Goal Sister Muscles

Encourage each other to do something that will make you feel stronger physically as well as mentally. For example, increase your exercise routine, take on a small home-repair project, sing out loud, walk up a steep hill, or move furniture around. You'll find that physical movement coupled with mental stretching can give you a great dose of energy with which to accomplish your goals.

Exercise 8.4: It's Me, but Stronger!

Find your trusty journal, any magazine you have in the house, scissors, and glue. Flip through the magazine and find three images or words that you would like to use to describe a stronger you. Glue these images or words onto a page in your journal. Beside each one, write two new physical ways in which you could embody that word. For example: "Brave" — "go up in a hot-air balloon" or "take a yoga class." Who knows, you might develop some new goals this way!

Practice What You Want to Get Better At

Ask your Goal Sister for her support as you focus on practicing new behaviors and actions. Instead of stewing about what you aren't doing well — or aren't doing at all — stop, breathe, and refuel. Ask her to remind you of the value of taking one step in an area in which you can be successful today. As the old saying goes, "Practice makes perfect." If you practice worrying and stewing, that is what you'll get better at!

Keep Believing in Each Other

When the chips are down, we need our Goal Sister more than ever! Having someone who will keep the faith when you're having a hard time believing in yourself is a huge relief. It frees you to place your attention on what matters most. Showing quiet confidence in your Goal Sister's abilities can take many forms. You can send her a thoughtful card and flowers or treat her to lunch or coffee one day this week. Making a quick phone call or e-mailing her a funny card can also do the trick.

Holding Each Other Accountable

It's the moment of truth! Did you do what you said you would do at your last Goal Sister meeting? Did your Goal Sister do what she said she'd do? Guess what? If you didn't do it, you didn't do it! No tomatoes will be thrown, and you won't be voted off the island. Instead, you will be accepted, gently questioned around the reasons for not meeting your goals, and encouraged to keep going.

Ann's Story

It was time for our weekly Goal Sister phone call. After Michelle and her family moved to Hawaii in 2002, we agreed to hold our monthly calls on the second Tuesday of every month, at 4:00 P.M. Missouri time and 11:00 A.M. Hawaii time. As we've been doing for many years, we share our progress toward our goals and we plan for our next month's accomplishments.

We'd been holding these monthly phone calls for a few months, but this time was different — at least it was for me. This time I had not completed all the steps toward my goals that I had set forth two meetings before. This time I was a little nervous about admitting that I wasn't the totally organized person I wanted to be. This time I knew that I would be letting my Goal Sister down by not having held up my end of the process. I began to compose the "right" explanation in my mind.

I dialed Michelle's number and she answered. "How's it going?" she asked. I offered up some lame conversation about how I was feeling stronger about a particular area of my life, and then she asked, "What about your goal to intensify your exercising?" Ugh. That was the one that got me.

"Well, I haven't done much on that one at all," I replied. "By the time I get home, I'm so tired that I can't think of doing anything but catching up on bill paying and straightening up the piles of books and papers in my office. And anyway, that new exercise tape is too long. I can hardly get through it." Then I braced myself for the lecture that I thought would come.

"Well, Ann, you know how much stress you have in your life right now. Don't you think you owe it to yourself to increase your exercise to balance out the stress?"

"Well, yes," I agreed, "but..."

"And aren't we both committed to increasing our exercise routine?"

"Yes, but..."

"So, let's both put more energy into making our exercise goals happen this month. I've been slipping, too, and I'm not very happy about it," said Michelle. "Maybe you could get up a little earlier in the mornings and do your eight minutes of weightlifting and twenty minutes with the exercise tape before you start your day. Then, later on in the day, you can go for a brisk walk. What do you think?"

"I think that sounds good," I responded, feeling relieved. "And how can I help you?"

"You can ask me in our Instant Message conversations if I exercised that day and how I felt. If I haven't exercised, I give you permission to jump on my case," said Michelle.

"Oh, okay. I can do that," I answered. "How about if we try it for one week and see how it goes?"

"Sounds like a plan," said Michelle.

That was it. Not too much badgering. Not too many disapproving comments. No accusations of failure. Just a reminder of our commitment, a couple of helpful suggestions, and a new plan to better keep on top of our exercise routines. That works for me!

A Goal Sister won't jump down your throat and attack you for not meeting your goals. But she isn't going to sit on the sidelines and let you slide, either. She remembers how important your goals are to you. She knows and trusts that you remember, too. So while she's willing to give you a break, she's not willing to let you forget the good experiences you deserve.

Turning Up the Heat

Being understanding and holding your Goal Sister accountable at the same time is a bit of a balancing act. You don't want to burn her for not stirring the pot of her goals as frequently as needed, yet you want to turn up the heat if her actions don't match her goals. This requires a high level of honesty between the two of you, while trusting each other's understanding of the situation. For example, you might turn up the flame when she tells you that she's researching new career options instead of calling potential employers. If, on the other hand, she has other irons on the fire, such as organizing a family gathering, training for a 5K run, or spending time with her children during their spring break, you might elect to let this particular goal simmer quietly. The two of you will decide on the best plan of action in the moment, based on what's cooking in her life. Return to the section entitled "Develop New Ways to Respond to Old Stressors" earlier in this chapter, and review those tips to apply here.

Ann's Story

As Michelle mentioned earlier, we've had fun using humor as a way to share some serious thoughts about our lives. During one of our Goal Sister trips, I found inspirational rocks with the word "create" on them. I bought one for each of us as a reminder that we're creating great lives. Michelle's rock also encourages her to get busy creating the art she's been wanting to put out into the world for a while. Here's a copy of an Instant Message exchange we had about her rock. It's an example of how I "turned up the heat" on her long-time goal.

AL: I know the holidays bring up this issue for me, but I'm afraid that you're going to die.

MBP: What?? Why?

AL: Because I'm looking at my "create" rock and remembering that yours says "create or die" — and you haven't created any artwork in a long time!

MBP: If you don't count doodling in my daily journal, you're right; I haven't created a thing. Thanks for reminding me.

AL: No problem. But we need to talk about your funeral, your wishes...

MBP: Okay, but can you hand me a tissue first?

AL: No, but I have a lovely red rose here; it will look nice lying across your breast in the coffin...

MBP: Box schmox! I'm going to be cremated!

AL: Whatever... do what you want. I'm still sending flowers.

MBP: Make them leis, ok?

AL: Well, DUH! Every guest will get one, too.

MBP: My, aren't we having a morbid conversation this morning?

AL: No, this isn't morbid. This is reality unless you get your ART BUTT in gear!

I love the fact that Michelle is open to this kind of exchange. She understands that, while we gently tease, we're both serious about doing what we say we want to do. It works, by the way. She has moved forward with creating great greeting cards and artwork for her home. Stay in touch; there is sure to be more of her work to come.

You've had quite a ride, Goal Sister. But moving through the stressful times helps you appreciate the good times even more.

Next time you meet with your Goal Sister, be sure to discuss the tips in this chapter and work with the ones that will be most helpful to you now. You may be in the early stages of getting to know each other; if so, it's important that you hear each other's reactions and stay on the same page. Whether you're new or old friends, your Goal Sister relationship will move you both forward with honesty, sharing, and support.

Chapter 8 Summary

★ As your Goal Sister friendship blossoms and you become comfortable working toward your goals together, it will become second nature to practice active listening, ask each other what you need, accept each other "as is," and show gratitude.

★ If you get frustrated or stuck, don't hesitate to ask your Goal Sister for help with problem solving. You might help each other navigate through your feelings about past mistakes or your limiting beliefs. It's okay to vent and ask for each other's assistance when you're stressed out!

★ One of the best gifts you can give yourself and your Goal Sister is permission to do what is needed on your path to goal achievement. Whether you need permission to stay stuck for a while, to ask for help when you're overwhelmed, to not beat yourself up, or to readjust your expectations, encourage each other to be exactly where you need to be in the process.

★ Take time to encourage your Goal Sister along her path. Giving and receiving love, acceptance, and encouragement can move you both forward to a better life.

★ Hold each other accountable for doing what you each said you were going to do. Whether you check in via a quick phone call or e-mail, report on your progress and gently question each other when you haven't met your goals. Encourage each other to keep going, help each other recommit to your goals, and problem-solve any obstacles.

Questions

★ *When is the last time you gave a word of encouragement to someone you care about?*

★ *How would you like your Goal Sister to keep you accountable for meeting your goals?*

Part III

Goals Will Keep Us Together

Chapter 9

Pack Your Bags for More Fun and Success!

There may come a time when it's impractical for you and your Goal Sister to meet in person as frequently as you once did. One of you may get a big project at work that will take up most of her time and attention for the next three months. One of you may move to another state, making it impractical to continue having twice-a-month in-person meetings. One of you may become ill for an extended period or be called upon for weeks to care for an ailing family member. Are these signs from the Universe that you should call it quits on your Goal Sister friendship? Heck no! We see them as invitations to flex your Goal Sister friendship muscles. To keep your friendship healthy and fit, we recommend that you maintain regular interactive communication about your goals and your progress. We suggest that you do this through a combination of in-person visits, phone calls, e-mail, and online chatting. We also strongly encourage you to go on overnight adventures with your Goal Sister.

What's an overnight adventure? We're glad you asked! After Ann moved from Illinois to Missouri, we took advantage of the physical distance between us to hold quarterly overnight meetings away from home. It was the most practical solution for our situation. We accomplished a lot in two-to-five-day trips filled with intense planning, reporting, and celebrating all that we'd accomplished. Sometimes we drove to our destinations, other times we hopped on airplanes. We mostly traveled to St. Louis and Rolla, Missouri, but we also held one quarterly meeting in Los Angeles. We stayed in motels or at the home of a good friend. We worked on our goals in hotel lobbies and restaurants, discussed our obstacles while swimming in pools, and problem-solved life's challenges while shopping for gifts to take home. We believe you can do it, too!

You don't need to move away from each other to hold overnight adventures. You might plan an overnight meeting to coincide with one of your birthdays, the latest attainment of a goal, or a conference or other event that you both want to attend. You might hold an overnight meeting when one of you needs extra support to get through a difficult transition. Perhaps the best reason to have an overnight adventure is to get away from your regular life to relax and refuel. And who better to do that with than your Goal Sister? A good rapport with — and understanding of — your Goal Sister is the foundation of this kind of adventure. Add the resources and time to make it happen, ask for help from supportive people to cover things at home, and you're set for a terrific twist to a Goal Sister meeting.

How Overnight Meetings Are Different

The focus of overnight meetings is still on setting goals, motivating each other, and solving problems. You and your Goal Sister will still follow the ten common courtesies listed in chapter 4, as well as sharing your stuff, exchanging gifts (if that's part of your standard repertoire), and having fun together. The difference is that you can do it over a span of a day or more, not just over lunch. This can be very freeing and productive. With that additional time, you and your Goal Sister can explore more facets of your goals, gain a deeper understanding of your personal blocks and limiting beliefs, and spread out discussions about ways to handle difficult situations. Overnight meetings also provide more opportunities to do visualization and self-help exercises together, to give each other feedback and suggestions about how to achieve difficult goals, and to get to know each other. More is definitely better in this case!

Getaway Details

When you decide to hold an overnight Goal Sister meeting, it's important to plan the event carefully. Where will you meet and for how long? Where will you stay? Can you afford it right now? These are the kinds of questions you and your Goal Sister will need to consider.

When, How Long, and Where?

We suggest that you schedule an overnight meeting at least twice a year; if you can afford it, hold one every three months. Be on the lookout for upcoming special events that you both want to attend. Maybe one of you needs to travel somewhere for work-related reasons and can meet with the other after her work obligations are completed. Based on your time and your budget, you and your Goal Sister can determine how often you'll schedule an overnight meeting.

The number of days you spend together often depends on the distance you must travel, the cost of the lodging, and your responsibilities at home. One night away is great, two nights is even better, and three nights is a luxury! We suggest that you start looking ahead in your calendars for chunks of time that you can take away from your regular life. Make sure you consider your loved ones' calendars as well when selecting your getaway dates.

Exercise 9.1: Hit the Road

Take a few moments to look at a map and note your favorite places, towns, and cities within a hundred-mile radius of where you both live. Consider places you've visited many times, as well as those you've been curious about exploring. Is there a day spa there? A great shopping center or a street full of antique malls? Maybe you've always wanted to stay at a certain lodge in a state park. Are there places that might stimulate your creativity or offer an experience related to achieving your priority goals? No matter what your interests, jot down those places you'd like to explore with your Goal Sister. Ask her to do the same, and see if you have some similar places in mind for a Goal Sister Getaway.

As you and your Goal Sister are deciding when and where to meet, you might want to consider how you to get to your destination. If you can travel together, you might be able to split the costs of getting there. If you're going to drive, make sure the car's in good working order! If you're traveling by bus or train, check the arrival and departure schedules; you don't want to spend too much of your overnight meeting time getting to and from your destination. If you're traveling by airplane, start saving your pennies and your mileage points.

Lodging is another factor to consider. We prefer to stay at motels that are off the beaten path. Use the Internet to find the best places to stay and the best deals available. Check out how previous motel guests rated the lodging and amenities (parking, on-site exercise room, indoor pool, coffeemaker, hair driers). Wherever you decide to stay, make sure you feel comfortable about your accommodations, that you'll be in a safe area, and that there's enough room to spread out and get a lot of work done.

Carry On!

When and where you go, how you get there, and what you plan to do there determines what items you should bring along. We suggest that you bring everything listed on page 62 under the heading "What to Bring." If you're traveling by car, bring your maps, favorite music and boom box, healthy snacks, anything to enhance your accommodations, your pillow, and food and drinks for your meeting. If you're traveling by bus, train, or airplane, your extra items will be limited by the size of your luggage. Don't forget to bring your swimsuit and camera!

Whew, does it really require all that planning and scheduling? Yes, it does, but it's worth the extra effort. It will get easier over time as you and your Goal Sister get into a rhythm of planning and scheduling your travel together.

Overnight Traditions

After all the planning, the scheduling, and the traveling to get to your destination, it's time to kick off your overnight meeting. We don't think you'll have a problem figuring out what to do together, but in case you're wondering, here are some things we like to do on our overnight adventures:

Eat, Drink, and Be Merry

For us, music is important. When we have our overnight meetings, we do our morning workouts to seventies' disco, listen to Broadway tunes as we get ready to go out for dinner, declare our goals with Prince, and relax with Enya. Sometimes we light candles and bring photographs of loved ones to display. We bring along our own serving dishes and glasses for in-the-room snacks and beverages, which helps us feel more at home. We take turns bringing snacks, and we have fun surprising each other with the variety of food we bring. It's a great opportunity to share new recipes and save money on eating out all the time. We bring our own alcohol and bottled water, and we basically move in for a great time of creating, sharing, and relaxing.

Schedule in Fun and Focus

We encourage you to plan for enjoyable activities during your overnight adventures. Swimming, walking, eating out, going to bookstores, shopping, and people-watching can do a lot to get your creativity flowing. Being away from your regular home and work life can do wonders for inspiring you to think, be, and act "outside the box." It also allows you the time to honestly assess what you want to create in your life. Plan some of your activities ahead of time, but leave room to be spontaneous once you get to your destination.

Like our regular Goal Sister meetings, we're pretty informal about when and where we talk about our progress toward our goals. We suggest you do whatever feels most comfortable to you. Some of you may need a bit more structure in your meetings. That's no problem! Simply take a few minutes after saying "hello" to determine what your priorities are and how you want to address them during your time together. For example:

ANN: I really want to talk about my money goals and my health goals first.

MICHELLE: Okay. I want to make sure we talk about my move to Hawaii and how we're going to stay in contact with each other.

ANN: And we have to go back to that bookstore.

MICHELLE: I agree! So why don't we go have dinner now and talk about your money goals? Then when we get back to the room, we can spend some time talking about my move. After a while, if we feel like swimming we can talk about our health goals in the pool. How does that sound?

ANN: That works. Tomorrow we can talk about more of our other goals. Let's head to the bookstore around 4:00, then go shopping afterward.

MICHELLE: Good. Grab your journal and let's go; I'm hungry!

The structure of your overnight meeting is influenced by the reasons you're getting together. If your meeting is focused on celebrating achievements, you may want to schedule in more fun around your goal-talking sessions. If your meeting is focused on relaxing and refueling, you may way to schedule in a massage or more quiet time together. Here's a story that illustrates how you and your Goal Sister can mix creativity and work during your overnight adventures.

Ann's Story

Michelle and I had many wonderful adventures during our overnight meetings. We took turns making the arrangements, and we always met at the agreed-upon time, ready for fun, sharing, and planning. I'm surprised that Michelle was willing to go on these trips, knowing her family responsibilities and her busy schedule, but I'm glad she did!

One of our memorable meetings was a spring trip to St. Louis, a city that offers great shopping and eating, as well as a variety of bookstores. Michelle got to the motel first and spread out her stuff on her side of the room. When I arrived, she helped me unload the cooler, suitcase, CDs, books, and pillows from my car. We fixed a drink, sank onto our beds, and began our meeting. My priority for our meeting was to have Michelle create drawings for my new business card.

No matter what we talked about or how many goals we planned for, Michelle constantly had a marker in her hand, drawing possible designs for me. We would get giddy and make up images that might work. She'd show me one design, and that would spark an idea for another. Somehow it all clicked. By the end of the next day, I had several designs that would serve me well. My part came when I got home and had to decide which ones would best represent my business!

Despite the creative pressure I had put on both of us during that trip, we still managed to have fun. Shopping for new planner pages, eating late at a great restaurant, and driving for miles in search of Mary Engelbreit's studio were all enjoyable parts of the trip. (We found Mary's studio, but no one was there. Darn!) I learned a lot about balancing work and play during that meeting. It is possible to have/be/do it all with your Goal Sister's support!

Sometimes your meeting will be focused on delving deeper into your personal blocks, brainstorming ways to increase your self-care, or giving each other extra support around hard-to-attain goals. Plan on exercising and taking other breaks that will energize you between your discussions.

Extra Nudging

Bring along self-help books that contain exercises to get you and your Goal Sister to think, feel, and act in bigger ways. Some of our favorites are Dave Ellis's *Falling Awake* and *Creating Your Future*. Doing the exercises in these books together and sharing your responses provide structure for your conversations about difficult issues, and it gives you the opportunity to nudge each other's limiting beliefs and behaviors.

Exchange Gifts

Another Goal Sister tradition that has an added twist during overnight adventures is the gift exchange. We put together gift bags containing stuff that we've stockpiled for each other since our previous quarterly meeting. We sometimes exchange gifts of drinking glasses and plates, knowing that we'll need them to drink the bubbly and eat the snacks we've brought along. Sometimes we wait to find the perfect gift for each other during our overnight adventure.

Ann's Story

We've held half a dozen Goal Sister meetings in Rolla, Missouri. It's about a two-and-a-half-hour drive from Joplin and a six-hour drive from Bloomington. We Midwesterners like to drive! We usually have productive meetings in Rolla because there's not much going on in town to distract us. Michelle and I found Zeno's, a motel where we like to stay every time; it has an indoor pool and the rooms are ample, with a table and two chairs. There's also a terrific restaurant and a gift shop with great jewelry.

In the fall of 2001, Michelle and I spent a fun-filled, productive weekend in Rolla. Halfway through our meeting, we took a break from discussing our goals and poked our heads into the gift shop. I spotted a really cool bracelet. I tried it on, and it was gorgeous. But I felt that it was out of my price range, so I resigned myself to admiring it from afar.

Michelle and I had a leisurely breakfast and worked on our next-quarter goals. We committed to achieving new goals related to our spending habits and to writing this book. When we finished up and we were ready to hit the road, I suggested that we take one more look at the bracelet. It was beautiful. Still, I had just committed myself to maintaining discipline in relation to my money goals. I swallowed hard and walked out of the store without my treasure. Michelle and I hugged good-bye, and off we went on our separate ways.

I was five miles down the road when I convinced myself to go back and buy the bracelet. Where would I find another like it? "If it's on my mind so much," I thought, "shouldn't I have it?" So I drove back to the motel.

I pulled in just as Michelle was coming out the motel side door.

"What are you still doing here?" I asked.

"Uh, I had to go to the bathroom again," she stammered,

eyes shifting from side to side. "What are you doing back here?" she demanded.

"I'm here to buy that bracelet!" I proudly declared.

"You can't do that," said Michelle. "You just set a goal not to spend any more money on things you don't need."

Just as smoothly, I delivered all of my rationalizations, certain that she would be amazed at how well I justified my decision.

"You can't go in there!" she exclaimed. "I just bought the bracelet for you! I was going to save it for a Christmas present, but you ruined the surprise." I stood there astounded, not believing my ears. Then she gave me the bracelet and I put it on. I kept shaking my head in amazement. "I know, I know, I am a sneaky, conniving friend," said Michelle. We both hugged good-bye for the second time and wished each other a safe journey home.

That gift was a surprise for me, and to this day it's a fun way for both of us to remember the trip and everything we accomplished and enjoyed together.

Declare Your Intentions

During your overnight meetings, we encourage you and your Goal Sister to declare your intentions. Declaring your intentions is a lot like stating your goals — but in this case, you scream them out to the world! It brings a different flavor to the proceedings.

Instead of simply writing your intentions in your journal, we suggest that you go to a place that has special meaning for you and publicly declare who you are or what you want to accomplish. Does this need to be done in a lecture hall before hundreds of people? No. Should you scream your intentions on a crowded bus? Not necessarily. It all depends on you and your situation.

Michelle's Story

Ann and I were in the midst of our spring 2000 quarterly meeting when Ann casually broached the subject of holding our fall meeting in Los Angeles. "It will be our way to cele-brate the millennium," she suggested. "We can declare our 2001 intentions to the ocean!" Without thinking of the practi-cal considerations, I agreed and imagined us walking together on the beach in Santa Monica, declaring ourselves boldly to the Pacific Ocean. Because this image was crystal clear in my mind, making the trip a reality didn't seem to be a big deal.

And it wasn't a big deal. We easily found four available days in our schedule, allowing for travel time. We received encouragement from our loved ones to proceed with the plans. We made airline reservations, using mileage points to pur-chase our tickets. We arranged for a rental car. My friend Phil invited us to stay with him and his family. Ann contacted her coach, Nancy, who lived in Los Angeles, and set up a lunch meeting.

Things continued to go well while we were in Los Angeles. We had the best time together, shopping, sharing goals, laugh-ing, scheming, people-watching, and discussing our initial ideas for this book. At one point, Ann reminded me, "Don't forget about declaring our intentions!" Then panic set in. "What am I going to say?" I asked myself over and over. We had lunch the next day with Ann's coach, Nancy, and told her about our plan to declare our intentions to the ocean. "What are you going to say?" asked Nancy. I mumbled something about being an artist. I felt the pressure building inside me as Ann and Nancy boldly stated their intentions for 2001 to each other. I smiled at them and finished my meal.

Later that day, I began badgering myself: "What is block-ing me from knowing what I need to say?" No clear answer came. The next morning, we went to the beach in Santa Monica and wrote down our next quarter's goals while sitting in the sand. I drew pictures in Ann's calendar as she declared her intentions. It was my turn. I sat, waiting for the words to come. "I am going to be... no, that sounds too wimpy... I want to be ... no, that's not right either." I stood up, brushed the sand off my legs, and said out loud, "I am a wife, mom, friend, Goal Sister, daughter, auntie, business owner, volunteer, believer, and artist." In that moment, I understood that I already am who I want to be. I needed to claim it and live it. For the rest of the world, it was just another moment, but for me it was a giant leap of faith.

Exercise 9.2: Something to Announce

You can declare your intentions much like we did. First, consider your list of goals and notice which ones could use a zestful kick in the pants. Is there a goal that keeps showing up on your list quarter after quarter, never getting the attention it deserves? Are you making a major shift in your thoughts or action about a particular goal? Choose the goals you'd really like to put out into the world. Next, get clarity about what you want to declare, and write it down. Use the present tense to make your declaration even more powerful. Examples include:

- "I am in a caring, trusting, supportive, committed intimate relationship with someone who appreciates me and doesn't take my love for granted!"

- "I take time every day to take care of me!"

- "I am climbing Mt. Fuji next summer with my best friend!"

- "I am releasing twenty pounds and buying new clothes to celebrate!"

Arrange to meet your Goal Sister in a public spot, preferably out in nature where you can really belt out your announcement. Center yourself and your confidence, then proclaim to the world who you are becoming.

The Goal Sister process will encourage you to stretch beyond your perceived limitations and to dream bigger than you had planned to dream. If you decide to declare your intentions with your Goal Sister, you'll find yourself stretching farther than you'd known you could.

Invite Creativity Along

Another tradition you might like to incorporate into your overnight meetings is drawing motivational pictures and phrases in each other's calendars and day planners. Having several days available to fill bigger sections of each other's calendar pages with words and images of support, motivation, and accountability is a gift that may set your inner creative beast free!

Michelle's Story

During our Goal Sister meeting in Los Angeles, I drew pictures of our experiences as they were happening. While we were resting in our room, I drew my version of the Santa Monica pier, our pal Sam the seagull, and Ann's favorite luxury hotel and bar, Shutters on the Beach. While we were generating goals on the beach, Ann mentioned all the people she felt grateful to have in her life. So guess what I did? I wrote that list of people next to a drawing I made of us lounging on the sand. It was a long list! While we were waiting to return our rental car, I scrawled "Life's a Beach" across the top of Ann's October 2000 calendar page and drew my memories of us talking about our goals, driving around in our rental car wearing our Goal Sister sunglasses, and people-watching on the Third Street Promenade. Ann appreciated having the

memories of our Los Angeles adventure on her calendar page;
I appreciated having the opportunity to create something
memorable and fun for my Goal Sister.

Whether you draw, play a musical instrument, knit, crochet,
or string beads, we encourage you to bring creativity along with
you on your overnight meetings. Doing something with your
hands often frees up your mind to think differently. It may also
help get you into a creative flow for generating goals and solving
problems. Your creative sky is the limit!

Slumber Parties

Sometimes your overnight meetings won't require that you go too
far from home. To save money and time, you might want to hold
a sleepover at one of your homes.

Goal Sister Group Story

In just eight weeks, the original Goal Sister group members
built support and rapport with each other. To celebrate the
conclusion of the pilot program, they decided to have a slum-
ber party, and they scheduled it so that Michelle could attend.
In addition to the regular topics of discussion, Michelle and
Ann wanted to use some of the group's time together to get
feedback on the Goal Sister concepts and process.

Ann suggested that they hold their slumber party over the
Kentucky Derby weekend, the first weekend in May. Joy took
the significance of the date a step farther and suggested that
they all wear hats, just as the Southern ladies would be doing
at the Derby. It was difficult to coordinate weekend schedules
to support a road trip, so they decided to camp out on Ann's
living room floor.

Michelle pulled in from Illinois early Saturday afternoon.
She and Ann went shopping for groceries and sticker supplies

for calendar pages, rearranged the furniture to make room for eight sleeping bags, and discussed the format of the gathering. At the appointed hour, the rest of the Sisters began to arrive with journals, books, pillows, sleeping bags, food, wine, and, yes, hats! Joy came ready for fun, dressed in beautiful pink pajamas and a matching robe that was perfectly accessorized with pearls and a great flowery hat. Deborah brought lots of chocolate for her fruit fondue, and Arlene brought chocolate-covered strawberries. You can never have too much chocolate! MJ arrived with a queen-sized air mattress, an old-fashioned hatbox, and several changes of clothing. There was much chatter and laughter as the other Sisters arrived. They passed around chips and dip, cookies, pretzels, and other snacks and got comfortable in Ann's living room as they caught up with each other about the latest goings-on.

The group members shared their impressions of the Goal Sister process and what makes it different from other friendships. Later, under a flashlight's glow, Ann led a discussion about childhood fears and how they influence us as adults. The group acknowledged the importance of having like-minded women to support them, and they visualized the creative process of getting this very book into the hands of the right publisher. They laughed and reflected, ate and drank, celebrated and created. Some of them even slept that night.

The next morning, they crawled out of their sleeping bags and groggily poured each other coffee and orange juice. Donning their hats, they toasted the Kentucky Derby and their wonderful breakfast. Nelda and Cindy sat bleary-eyed, not wanting to talk about goals until the coffee kicked in. MJ frowned at her air mattress, which had slowly deflated overnight. The Goal Sisters wrapped up their morning meeting by sharing their priority goals for the upcoming quarter, saying their good-byes to Michelle, and basking in their time away from their regular routines. It was a great meeting!

Ann continued to facilitate monthly Goal Sister group meetings; then group members decided to have another slumber party six months later to get their new year off to a productive, fun start. They held this second slumber party on a weekend in January when Michelle and MJ (who had both moved to Hawaii by then) were visiting the mainland.

Goal Sister Group Story

Ann informed the Sisters that the focus of their second overnight meeting would be on developing their New Year's goals. Little did the others know that Ann and Michelle had just signed a contract with a publisher for this book; Ann and Michelle agreed that the original Goal Sister group should be the first to hear the news. Dinner at a local restaurant was arranged to kick off the overnight meeting. Wine was ordered. Ann raised her glass in a toast to the get-together, then added that they were also celebrating a new book contract. Talk about shocked looks, squeals of delight, and hearty applause! Ann and Michelle told their story about how they'd found their publisher. The Sisters were thrilled with the news and were glad to know that other women, like you, would soon be benefiting from living the Goal Sister process.

After celebrating at the restaurant, they headed back to Ann's place and took turns reviewing the previous year and the events that had taken place. Ann got everyone thinking about different people who had influenced them, any regrets they had, and any negative habits they'd let go of. As midnight approached, the Sisters found their spots on the floor, spread out their sleeping bags, and fell asleep.

The next morning, Ann woke everyone up early with her "chop chops," as there was a lot left to cover on the agenda. The Sisters talked about their goals for the upcoming year, then they created treasure collages to serve as visualizations of their written goals. There were magazines everywhere, and scissors were clipping crazily as they each found exactly the right images. "If anyone sees the word 'goal' I want it!" came a request, and then a few minutes later, "Who wanted the word 'goal'? I found one." This happened repeatedly as each woman sought images to represent travel, relationships, business success, exercise, and fun. It was another enjoyable, productive overnight meeting.

The Sisters shared their completed collages with each other at their next monthly meeting. Cindy's was full of travel images and pictures of her Goal Sisters on the Oprah Winfrey Show. *MJ had created a great collage of her dual life in Hawaii and Missouri. Nelda's collage focused on a healthy lifestyle and getting herself organized. Joy's images expressed a refreshed living environment. Karen shared a notebook she'd created, with a picture of her goal for each category on its own page.*

Then came Deborah's treasure collage. One of the first things that jumped out of it was the word "Love." "I think I'm ready to consider a relationship in my life," she quietly declared. In previous meetings, Deborah had shared her fear of commitment in an intimate relationship, based on a failed marriage and a couple of other relationships that hadn't worked out. She'd been adamant about the new standards she would set for any potential suitors, letting her Goal Sisters know that she wasn't in any hurry to get into a new relationship. So they were surprised when she softly said, "I think it would be nice to have a companion to share my life with now."

They were excited by this shift, and they joined in with their ideas of the perfect someone for Deborah. They devised wonderful ways for them to meet and imagined the first conversation they would have. They generally reverted to high school as they schemed, wished and hoped that her newly opened heart would be richly rewarded.

Days after the meeting, Deborah put her treasure collage on her refrigerator. Every day, she saw it when she searched for a snack, a cold drink, or some fruit. Every day, the image of love nestled a little closer to her heart. Without any real prospects, it was going to be fun to see how this one played out. But there was a man named Gene, with whom she worked off and on. They had been friends for years, creating artwork together and sharing an occasional dinner.

One day in February 2003, Gene announced that he was quitting his job and moving to California in search of new opportunities. Deborah was supportive, and she began to encourage her friend in his changes. Their conversations got a little deeper, they spent more time together, and sparks of love began to glow. They both knew that their friendship wasn't meant to end. Then Gene made sure of that with a marriage proposal — and Deborah said "yes"! They're now making plans for a New Year's wedding and a move to California.

"You know, I think it was the treasure collage that did it," says Deborah. "You ask for something, you're willing on some level to have it, and God provides it. This is so cool!"

You don't need a book contract, birthday, job promotion, or other special reason to have a slumber party and to create a visualization of your goals. In fact, you don't need a reason at all! You and your Goal Sister will decide together when to take a break from your lives to have an overnight adventure that includes more time to work on your goals and more opportunities to be creative together.

Exercise 9.3: A-Visualizing We Will Go

To make your own treasure collage, gather up old magazines, scissors, glue, and a piece of poster board. Make sure you have your priority goal list in front of you. Put on some music and find a comfortable chair or spread out on the floor. Go through the magazines and cut out positive words and pictures that depict your goals. You might find pictures of people doing what you want to do, like camping, speaking to a group, or exercising. You might search for pictures of things you want to have, like a new desk, a car, or a house. You might choose to include motivating phrases like "delivers value," "drink that water," or "worth a million!"

Once you've collected your words and images, arrange them as a collage on your poster board. We like to put a deadline in the center, like "by July 31, 2005" or "2005," then add the phrase "this or something better." When you've finished your treasure collage, hang it where you'll see it every day. Ann's collage is in her bedroom where she sees it every time she wakes up and before she falls asleep. Michelle's collage is in her office over her desk. As you look at your treasure collage, spend a few moments visualizing how it's going to feel to have these things in your life. See them happening to you now, and give thanks for them.

Staying Connected to Loved Ones at Home

For most of us, the opportunity to have an overnight meeting with our Goal Sister is a luxury. Whether your role is that of mother, partner, pet owner, or caregiver, going away may mean that someone else is missing you or temporarily covering your responsibilities.

Ann's Story

When I look back on our years as Goal Sisters, I'm amazed at all that Michelle and I have created in our time together.

Most rewarding for me, though, is the commitment we made to get together on a regular basis. I have a lot of really good friends, but I don't know many who would travel hundreds of miles to get together for a few intense days of supporting each other in designing a great life. That's exactly what Michelle and I did after I moved from Illinois to Missouri, and after she and her family moved from Illinois to Hawaii.

Nor do I know a lot of families who would understand and accept that part of the process for their mom/wife/partner. Michelle's husband, Bart, is one of those rare men. He saw the value to both of us of spending time together in Goal Sister sessions. He supported our efforts, and he did so at great sacrifice. While I had fewer obligations to meet (making arrangements for two cats was my biggest challenge when we had overnight meetings), Michelle had to seek support in handling the kids' obligations, meal preparation, and the details of daily living. Bart was willing to rearrange his work schedule and become the master chef and chauffeur in order to accommodate the kids' schedules, as well as ours, when Michelle and I went away overnight. I'm really grateful to Bart — and happy that Michelle has that kind of support for realizing her dreams.

If you have loved ones who'll be missing you while you're away, take time during your overnight meeting to call home and let them know how you're doing and how your work is coming. They appreciate being included in the process, and they'll be relieved to know that you've arrived safely and are enjoying your time together. Be sure to thank them for helping to make that happen! Expressing your gratitude for their support will go a long way toward helping them feel appreciated, valued, and involved in the great life you are creating.

Exercise 9.4: Parting Is Such Sweet Sorrow

As you plan for your overnight Goal Sister adventure, take some time to communicate your love and appreciation to those you're temporarily leaving behind. You might write a card for each family member and leave them in places where they'll discover them while you're gone. You might leave a personal e-mail message letting friends and coworkers know when you'll return home or be back in the office. If you feel that someone in particular will miss you while you're at your overnight meeting, take the time before you leave to do something special for that person.

Bringing Yourself and Your Goals Home

As we've said before, be sure to record your goals before you leave your meeting. Overnight meetings are no exception. We usually do this over breakfast on our last day together. We take out our notebooks or journals and ask each other about each of the goal categories. As usual, write down both your own goals and your Goal Sister's goals so that you can gently hold each other accountable throughout the coming weeks.

Before you go, be sure to review your time together and talk about the parts that energized you and gave you a new perspective. Discuss how you want to return to your regular life. How will you start tomorrow to work on the goals you've identified for yourself today? Also, decide how and when you'll communicate next. End with a big hug and a thank-you. We always end by saying "Onward and upward!" That's where you're headed too, Goal Sister. Your continued willingness to embrace this process will bring you great rewards, at home and away.

Chapter 9 Summary

★ It might not be convenient for you and your Goal Sister to meet as often as you did at first. Let yourselves experience Goal Sister meetings in a different way by having an overnight adventure. Schedule in fun and focus as you plan where you'll meet and how long you'll stay.

★ With the additional time allowed by overnight meetings, you and your Goal Sister can explore more facets of your goals, gain a deeper understanding of your personal blocks, and have longer discussions about how to handle difficult situations.

★ Overnight meetings also provide more opportunities to do visualization and self-help exercises together, to give each other feedback and suggestions about how to achieve difficult goals, and to get to know each other.

★ For overnight meetings, in addition to the activities that make your regular Goal Sister meetings productive and fun, start new traditions by sharing your favorite snacks and drinks, bringing along your favorite music, and declaring your intentions together.

★ Invite creativity along by decorating each other's day planners with reminders of important deadlines and commitments. Add color and use stickers for extra impact. You might consider making a treasure collage of your goals as another way to have creative fun and visualize your goal achievements.

★ You may want to hold a slumber party instead of traveling away from home. This doesn't cost as much or take too much time away from your regular lives.

★ If your overnight adventure takes you away from loved ones, check in with them while you're gone, and show your gratitude to the ones who are covering your responsibilities.

Questions

★ *What kind of overnight adventure would you like to take with your Goal Sister?*

★ *How can you tap into your creativity during your overnight meeting?*

Chapter 10

Continuing Together on the Path of Success

Many things can happen that make it challenging to maintain success in some areas of your life. New routines you've established may become boring. Family members or friends may feel uncomfortable with your newfound success and try to bring you back to the old status quo by sabotaging your efforts. You may experience a big change in your life that takes away your focus on your goals. Take heart, Goal Sister; our process can help you manage these challenges and sustain your achievements.

Helping Each Other Maintain Success

It's natural to encounter setbacks when you work toward your goals over the long haul. Sometimes the setbacks are temporary. For example, your church might be short on volunteers for a community project; you might be asked to help out at the same time you're planning to catch an exercise class. Or your best friend calls needing your support right now, but you're working to meet a deadline. At other times, the setbacks can be longer lasting, like when your child is sick with the flu and you miss a week of your music lessons, or you witness a terrible accident and you have difficulty concentrating on anything for days afterward. As a result of such setbacks, your efforts toward goal achievement can fade away.

Michelle's Story

One of the best experiences I left behind when we moved away from Bloomington, Illinois, was the fitness routine that had taken me several years to establish. I took land aerobics three to four times a week at the Workout Company, where I had wonderful instructors and fun people to exercise with, and water aerobics two to three times a week at the YWCA, where I worked out with a lively group of mostly older women. I was on a low-fat, high-carbohydrate diet. I completed a fitness journal every day. By the time we moved, I had maintained my fitness goals for three years and had lost almost thirty pounds.

When we began our cross-country trip, I started lapsing in regard to my health goals. It became harder to eat the way I was used to eating. We camped for most of our trip, so making oatmeal over a campfire wasn't practical. Exercising at the intensity I was accustomed to was also out of the question. I told myself that this was only temporary, and that I'd get back to meeting my health goals as soon as we got to Hawaii.

Boy, was I wrong. Not only did I not exercise when we got to Hawaii, but I started making a daily habit of eating all the food I'd grown up with! I especially pigged out on mahimahi plate lunches, which include two scoops of rice and a scoop of macaroni salad. This wasn't healthy for me! So, you guessed it, I began gaining back the weight.

When I spoke with Ann about my frustration, she helped me see that I needed to stop beating myself up. She reminded me that my family and I had gone through a lot of changes — and were still doing so — and that it was natural for me to lapse in regard to some of my goals. Then Ann asked me, "What are you going to do now?" I joined a new gym and tried to resume some of my old healthy habits. After a series of false starts, I ended up sidelined for two months with an arm injury.

I wanted to scream and give up! But instead I called Ann. She encouraged me to take care of my arm and figure out other ways to exercise in the meantime. I purchased fitness tapes online and started working out with them. They were fine, but I didn't feel much better, nor did I lose any weight. So I enrolled at the YMCA, and now I'm taking land and water aerobics classes there. The people there are friendly, and the instructors are tough and encouraging.

I'm slowly getting back into shape with my new fitness routine, and I'm cutting back on eating my favorite local foods. I know it's going to take time. Thank goodness Ann is there to support me and to show me through her own fitness routine that it can be done. I now have a new health goal: My high school reunion is coming up, and I plan to attend as a fit Michelle!

We encourage you and your Goal Sister to hang in there when either of you lapses in your efforts to achieve your goals. It may be helpful to suggest new routines or modify existing ones that previously got the results you wanted. Either way, it's a crucial time for Goal Sisters to be supportive of each other.

Another way to help each other maintain success is to continue keeping each other accountable. Whether your Goal Sister has lapsed on her goal achievement or is working toward a goal that involves a habit that's hard to break, it's important to keep her accountable to the goals she has set for herself.

Michelle's Story

Every New Year's Day, my friend of fifteen years calls and tells me about all her accomplishments over the past year. For the past four years, Darlene hasn't had much good news to share about her money goals. I'm not sure why her money goals are so daunting, but they are and she hasn't made much progress on them.

For the past four New Year's Days, Darlene has vowed to change how she manages her money: This is the year she's going to set up a budget, this is the year she's going to pay off her credit cards, and this is the year she's going to spend within her means. Whenever Darlene states these intentions, I believe her and encourage her because I want her to succeed. But within a month, Darlene usually goes overboard in her spending and doesn't bring up her money goals until the next New Year's Day.

Like clockwork, Darlene called me this past January first to tell me about all her accomplishments from last year. Then she made her commitments for this year. When she got to the subject of money, I listened and told her that I supported her in achieving her goals. So what did Darlene do the following week? She threw an extravagant birthday party for a friend! She told me about all the things she bought for the party: the decorations and party favors, the food and drinks, the birthday card and the gifts. She told me how much fun everyone had at the party, especially the guest of honor. Darlene enjoyed telling me about all these details, which made it even tougher to say, "Sounds like it was a great party, but how much did it cost you?" She hemmed and hawed, then gave me an excuse about wanting to make her friend's birthday a celebration to remember because she hadn't had much joy in her life recently. Darlene added, "Plus, it's not like I paid for a hotel suite; the party was at my house. Just think of all the money I saved by having it here!"

At this point in our conversation, I had two distinct paths I could take: the well-worn path where I would say nothing about Darlene's actions not lining up with her words, or the path less taken, where I would call Darlene on the fact that her actions were out of alignment with her goals. I decided to take the latter path and said, "You have a big heart, Darlene. You are kind and thoughtful. Everyone we know appreciates you for your caring and generosity." I paused, took a deep breath, then continued, "That said, I'm worried that you can't afford to pay for the kind of party you just threw for your friend. I'm confused when you continue to tell me that you want to change your spending habits, then proceed to spend your money in ways that you can't afford."

"I know, I know," lamented Darlene. "It's just that..." And then I listened to Darlene give me all her excuses for not living from her intentions. When she was through, I said, "I don't want to criticize you, and I don't want to judge you. I want to support you, but I don't know how to best do that right now. If your spending behavior is truly something you want to work on, then I support you 100 percent in doing that. If you're not ready to work on your money goals and you just want to state them every New Year's Day without taking any meaningful action toward them, then I support you 100 percent in doing that. But I need to know: Which way do you want me to support you?" Darlene was silent for a long time. "Let me think about it and get back to you."

Darlene did get back to me in a week, and she asked me to support her in taking steps toward achieving her money goals. She told me that our conversation had made her angry, but that it woke her up to seeing how much her actions weren't aligned with her stated intentions. Darlene defined a few Small Goals that she could achieve to make progress toward her bigger money goals. We agreed to check in with each other every month. Darlene hasn't yet achieved all of her money goals, but she is taking more steps forward than backward, and I applaud her for it.

Goal Plateaus

Sometimes you and your Goal Sister may experience some success with a goal, then feel that you've stalled in your progress. If you're like us, you may want to see more results and get discouraged when nothing you do seems to make a difference. At such times, we suggest that you talk openly with your Goal Sister about your feelings and be receptive to hearing feedback.

Goal Sister Group Story

When the Goal Sisters look back on their first group meeting, they all share a good laugh. They had no idea how far they would come as individuals and as a group. At the first meeting, Nelda's body language spoke volumes about her comfort level: Crossed arms and legs held the Sisters at bay. Deborah's reserve told them that she would "wait and see." MJ's release of feelings about her then-recent divorce told the Sisters that there was a need for emotional processing.

The women slowly began to build trust with each other and gain confidence in themselves. They listened to each other and told each other the steps they would take to achieve the successes they desired. They motivated and nudged each other, celebrated and shared together. Little by little, they began to adapt the Goal Sister process to their own lives.

Then they began to experience setbacks in working toward their goals. Sometimes they felt frustrated over not having accomplished the goals they'd set for the previous month. Sometimes they were afraid that they'd expected too much of themselves too quickly. Sometimes they took little or no action toward their goals. Whatever the reasons, the Sisters experienced setbacks.

Over time, the Sisters learned that setbacks are part of the process, and that they can overcome them. When one Sister shared her disappointment in herself, the others responded in true Goal Sister fashion. Their responses ranged from being understanding ("It's a busy time for you right now, and that's okay") to asking for accountability ("Hey, you've had this goal for two months and nothing's happened; what's up?"). They quickly learned that the monthly meeting was a time to address progress as well as feelings of being stuck on their paths to success.

You might feel discouraged when nothing you do seems to make a difference. At such times, we suggest that you consider the distinction between "doing" and "being" your goals, as illustrated in Ann's next story.

Ann's Story

I was enjoying a conversation with a good friend who does intuitive readings. Shane always provides me with food for thought, and I usually walk away from our conversations shaking my head in disbelief. This day was no exception.

Shane did a great job of tuning in to the success of the book you are now reading. He also gave me valuable insights about my primary relationship, and he provided the right take on a friend's health situation.

Then I asked him about my career and financial goals. I was curious about why I hadn't made any progress with them over the previous few months. I was enjoying steady income and a regular clientele, but despite increasing my speaking engagements and mailing a large number of business post-cards, I was not attracting more clients to help increase my income. I would get calls of inquiry, but no one new would commit to a regular coaching contract.

Shane smirked. It was a friendly smirk — the kind that told me I was about to get a lesson with a powerful message, whether I wanted it or not. "I would say that you haven't ever stayed at a plateau in your life," he guessed. "I would say that you are so busy doing and growing and moving that you wouldn't know what it is like to be still."

BAM! POW! ZAP! Holy lightning bolt, Batman! He was

right. My ears perked up to hear his explanation. "You don't like things to be static. You're in constant movement. If your bank account isn't growing as you think it should, you think you must be getting deeper into debt. If you aren't losing weight, you figure you must be gaining it. If your relationship isn't progressing as quickly as you think it should, then it must be headed for disaster. This plateau is where you need to be, and you need to accept the fact that you are there," Shane asserted.

It's true. I had always been on the go and wanting results now. As a Goal Sister, that has been a good thing; I can motivate others and be motivated by someone with the same enthusiasm. Yet more and more I am learning that there's a different kind of action in waiting and just being. Does that make sense? When we are still, our minds don't totally stop; our thoughts continue to create our world. So by thinking about a desired outcome, you're in the process of creating it in each moment — whether you're sitting on the couch or making that presentation to your management team.

Goal plateaus can remind us about the balance between "doing" our goals and "being" our goals. That's a big distinction. Acting as if the end result has already occurred can help you get closer to achieving your goal. It doesn't mean that you spend days and days in the planning stage. "Being" is different. "Being" is acceptance. "Being" means having neither judgment nor expectations. "Being" can be difficult, but the new experience of accepting yourself "as is" is progress in and of itself.

Exercise 10.1:
Your Best- and Worst-Case Scenarios

To get an idea of your best- and worst-case scenarios for your goals, take out your journal and write each of your current priority goals at the top of a new page. Draw a vertical line down the center of the page, extending from your goal statement to the bottom of the page. On the left-hand side of the line, write three worst-case scenarios — what could happen or how you would feel if you didn't accomplish this goal. On the right-hand side of the line, write three best-case scenarios of what you want to have happen or how you'll feel when you accomplish this goal.

Take a few moments to quietly reflect on which side of the line your current status leans toward. Now answer these questions in your journal:

- If, from this moment on, I neither progressed nor backslid in relation to this priority goal, would it be all right?
- If I wouldn't be okay with that, what is one small step I could take tomorrow toward accomplishing this priority goal?
- If I am okay with not progressing, how can I reward my acceptance?
- What can I do or tell myself today that will help me accept where I am?

Here's an example of Michelle's worst- and best-case scenarios:

Play Goal: Lighten Up with My Kids	
Worst-Case Scenarios	Best-Case Scenarios
Take out my frustrations on Zoë and Kanoa.	Pinpoint where my frustrations are coming from and deal with them.
Be a mom who always pops off the handle.	Be mindful about my reactions to my kids' misbehavior.
Don't make any time to play.	Have regular playtime with my kids.

When Big Change Happens

Can you use the Goal Sister process when you or your Goal Sister experiences a really big change in your lives? The answer, dear Goal Sister, is a resounding "yes!" It's likely to happen: One of you may move across the country, one of you may start or end a relationship, one of you may have a baby, one of you may change careers. The key to maintaining your sisterly bond during times of big change involves building on the strengths of your friendship and responding in a creative way.

Communicating your needs to your Goal Sister is essential during times of big change. Together you can design a response plan that will serve you both and provide the much-needed support that the Sister-in-transition needs. We suggest that you consider including the following actions in your plan:

- Increase your level of encouragement. Sending a funny e-card or thoughtful note can mean a lot to her.

- Express your support verbally. A quick "hang in there!" phone call can help.

- Normalize her stress levels: "Hey, Goal Sister, it's okay. Most people in your situation would be feeling the same way."

- Give her permission to put her goals on hold for a while. She may feel that she's not only letting herself down, but letting you down as well.

- Acknowledge frustration and other feelings. A friendly "Gee, you're sure calling a lot lately. I'm in the middle of meeting a big deadline, so can we set a time to talk later?" can protect your time and energy as well as hers.

- Brainstorm with your Goal Sister to discover other helpful people in her life who she can turn to and rely on for support.

- Remind each other to use strategies that can calm and center you both, including exercising, journaling, meditating, gardening, playing with your pets, and listening to music.

- Adjust your communication patterns. Accept the fact that your Goal Sister may need to vent or stress out for a while, requiring more or less frequent contact. Work together to set limits if necessary.

These are the times that can test your Goal Sister friendship. Yet the reality is that you can use your friendship to get through the tough times. It's important to remind yourself that you can empathize with your Goal Sister while remaining focused on what you need to do for yourself. These transition times give you and your Goal Sister an opportunity to use a different repertoire of coping responses. Whether these big changes are a result of life "happening to you" or are eagerly desired, communicating with each other and designing a coping plan together may ease the stress.

Michelle's Story

It's not a coincidence that MJ and I became closer after I moved to Hawaii in 2002. Sure, we both live in Hawaii, but MJ lives on Kauai, which is a twenty-minute flight and a $132 round-trip ticket away from Oahu, where I live. Sure, we're both Goal Sisters, but we only met in person three times prior to MJ's moving to Kauai. If you look at our lives, we don't seem to have much in common: MJ grew up in the Midwest and I grew up in Hawaii; MJ is eight years younger than me; MJ is happily single and I'm happily married.

But you can't judge a book by its cover; MJ and I have a lot in common. We both moved to a tropical place where the time zone is five to six hours behind the majority of our friends. We're also both in the process of making big changes in our lives: MJ is embarking on a brand-new life with a brand-new career, and I'm living my dream to be a writer and artist. It's scary stuff, believe us! And most people we know don't completely understand why we're doing what we're doing. Up close, they admire us; from afar, they think we are nuts! Most days we feel confident about our choices. But if someone's comment should jar us ("So, tell me again, you scuba-dive and what else?") or fill us with doubts ("What are you going to do after you write the book?"), it helps to have each other there to provide support. As MJ once said, "When nothing makes sense, I have someone to call."

In addition to being in the same time zone, the best part of our friendship is that we don't feel compelled to know every detail of each other's lives. We call each other for support, and we e-mail each other our prayers and thoughts when either of us is going through a tough time. We're planning to hold our first shared Goal Sister adventure soon. I'm looking forward to spending more time with MJ and having more opportunities to learn from each other. Our friendship is an unexpected surprise for both of us — and it's a friendship we're both committed to keeping!

Exercise 10.2: Cope, Don't Mope

How do you cope when the chips are down? Louise Hay, a self-help author who spoke at a conference Ann attended many years ago, told a story about a friend who had a unique way of coping with stress. This friend taped an index card to her bedroom alarm clock that said "peaceful and joyful." When questioned about the card's purpose, the friend replied, "I would rather wake up feeling peaceful and joyful than alarmed!"

How about you, Goal Sister? Have you given thought to

how you would like to "wake up" to your life? How will you cope with life's challenges? Take a few minutes now to close your eyes, take a deep breath, and imagine how you will feel tomorrow when the new day greets you. Will you feel excited? Enthusiastic? Calm and confident? Get out ten index cards or sticky notes, and record one feeling you would like to have on each card or note. Carry the cards with you and review them throughout the next week, or stick them up around your home where you'll see them frequently. The bathroom mirror is a great place to put some. These words are a gentle reminder that you can choose a different response to life's stressors. Share your word images with your Goal Sister at your next meeting. Go ahead: Respond to your stress differently, and reap the benefits!

Extra Nudging

Pay attention to how you're responding to big changes in your life. Whether you're making these changes deliberately or something stressful is happening to you, you might be tempted to temporarily turn to food, sex, drugs, or alcohol for immediate relief. If that's true, try to replace that behavior with other behaviors you've used in the past to cope with stress. Praying or meditating might help. Exercising or playing a musical instrument might also work as coping responses. Seek counseling if you feel that you need more intensive help.

Speaking Your Truth

One of the hardest yet most freeing actions you can take with your Goal Sister is what we call "speaking your truth." This requires you to be clear about your values, strong in your integrity, and certain of your voice. Why? Your opinion matters to your Goal Sister. When you offer it, you want to make sure you're being honest and clear with her. Remember, she already has other friends and family who will tell her what she wants to hear; she is relying on you to speak your truth. When either of you faces a plateau or begins to cope with a big change, your honesty can help you both meet it with more grace.

Where do you find your truth? Aisle ten at the grocery store? On sale at your favorite retail outlet? At the movie theater? No. Your truth is found within you. It comes from your soul; if you listen, it will guide you to the right action and words — that is, the right action and words for *you*. Your truth is yours alone. The challenge is to speak it honestly without imposing it on your Goal Sister (or anyone else, for that matter). We ask that you be candid with yourself about your feelings regarding your Goal Sister's plateau, big change, or goal choices. Here are examples of ways in which you can speak your truth and respect her feelings:

- "I want to tell you something that may be hard for you to hear."

- "My intention is not to hurt your feelings, but to tell you how I see things."

- "I want to tell you something, and I'm concerned about how you're going to take it."

- "I worry about you when..."

Speaking your truth is just that. In other words, once you express yourself it's time to let go of your expectations about her response. This can be very difficult! We secretly want our Goal Sister to awaken from her slump, say, "Oh yes! You're so right! What was I thinking?" and go back to being the terrific, level-headed person we've always known. That could happen. But also prepare yourself for other responses.

It's your Goal Sister's right to say, "Thank you for speaking your truth, but I feel that I'm on track with where I want to be." Or "I hear your concerns and I'll use some of your suggestions, but I'm not going to do them all." As you each get better at speaking your truth, you can also get better at releasing your expectations about the results. This can take your friendship to a new level that's even more fulfilling. It can also give you more confidence in yourself and how you see your world.

Ann's Story

We all have days when there's so much on our plate that we're feeling stressed. We read the magazine articles and hear the TV talk-show hosts instructing us to prioritize and delegate our many tasks. I was no doubt in one of those periods of my life, but I wanted all of it! Writing more articles for magazines, writing this book, reaching out to new coaching clients, maintaining friendships, exercising regularly, exploring a new romantic relationship, and assisting in creating a new nonprofit organization were all things I wanted in my life. I was enjoying the variety of projects in my life, and I believed that I was balancing them all easily. Michelle did not.

At the same time, my friendship with a new man in my life was deepening. We very naturally developed trust, respect, and love for each other. I was happy. It was wonderful to find someone with whom to share and express more of my beliefs about life. And I wanted to share my excitement with my Goal Sister.

Each time there was a glimmer of hope for a romantic relationship, it was my Goal Sister I wanted to share it with. Likewise, when outward appearances were in conflict with my inner knowing, I wanted to hear her thoughts. I was in the awkward stage between doubt and trust, fear and confidence, and I needed assurance that I was on the right track — not only with this new relationship, but in the rest of my life as well.

Around that time, Michelle let me know that she wanted to have a phone conversation to "talk about something pretty important." We set a time to talk, and I began to wonder what was on her mind. Had she decided to abandon her goals and pursue another direction? Had she been given bad news by a doctor? Or maybe she needed my thoughts on how to respond to something one of the kids had done or said? I didn't know, but I was open to hearing whatever she had to say.

"I have to say something, and I don't want to hurt your feelings," she began. Then, through words that were sometimes harsh, most times gentle, Michelle let me know that she felt I was putting too much energy into my new relationship. She thought I was getting too caught up in the emotions, at the cost of my other work and friendships. She didn't want our conversations to focus solely on this new relationship, although it sounded like she was saying she didn't want to have any part in these conversations for much longer.

At first I was devastated: "If I can't share everything with my Goal Sister, then who can I talk to?" I had put a lot of energy into this special bond with Michelle, and finding that I had possibly misjudged it really stung. Through prayer, I became able to hear Michelle's concerns, examine her observations, and check in with my own perceptions of reality. Because I loved Michelle, I respected her opinion. I had to work hard to respect and trust mine just as much.

The upshot is that Michelle and I are working through it and respecting each other's limits around this topic of conversation. I still share updates about the new relationship, but I'm careful not to go on and on about it. This is part of the Goal Sister friendship: learning the safe spots and the uncomfortable ones, and enjoying that journey together. I'm thankful that Michelle cares enough about me to voice her concerns. I know I'd do the same for her.

Michelle's Story

The phone call Ann's referring to was one of the hardest I've ever made. She's right; I was worried about her putting too much energy and focus into a relationship that, from my perspective, wasn't close to being the right one. It was hard to see her shift her focus from her coaching/training/writing business to other interests. In addition, Ann had recently ended a significant relationship, and my memories of the tough times she endured had not faded. I believed I had reasons to be concerned for her.

I felt like an ogre for making the call. I knew that my opinion would dampen her excitement over her new relationship and affect our Goal Sister friendship. I was afraid of hurting her feelings. I was afraid she would out-and-out disagree with my perspective. I was afraid to be the friend who spoke her truth.

But Ann didn't yell or hang up on me. She was pretty quiet, and she said she was being open and taking it all in. When I asked her if anything I'd said made sense, Ann initially said "no." She was happy with the way things were, and she felt just as committed to our Goal Sister friendship and to her work as she'd ever been. She got pretty tearful, and at the end of our conversation she thanked me. Several days later, Ann called to tell me which parts of my concerns made sense to her and which parts didn't. She told me that she was grateful for our friendship and knew that my concerns were coming from a place of caring.

I'm glad I spoke my truth. Although Ann and I still disagree about the choices she's making, our conflict has brought us closer and helped us clarify our beliefs and our course of action. We continue to be honest, we continue to support each other, and we continue to respect each other's path. We have not abandoned our Goal Sister friendship over this disagreement, because our relationship is too important to both of us.

Extra Nudging

When you feel the need to speak your truth, you might want to write your thoughts in your journal and sort them out before you express yourself verbally to your Goal Sister. After doing that, give yourself a day or two before you go back to review what you've written. Figure out which parts are rants and which parts are feelings you want to express. You may want to take some additional time to refine your feelings and make sure they're in alignment with your values before you speak your truth.

Exercise 10.3: Truth or Dare?

Remember that childhood game? Play it again now, but differently. This time, rather than taking the dare to do some outrageous task, dare to be honest with yourself. Take out your journal and review your latest list of goals. Ask yourself if you're withholding a truth about each of them. For example, in your "money" category, you might think: "I'm withholding my truth by acting like I can make my monthly credit card payment without any problem. I need to call the company, be honest about my situation, and make alternative payment arrangements." As you discover your truth, write a new list of goals in your journal; next to each one, write your feelings about it and the action you will take toward expressing your truth.

Exercise 10.4: Dropping Names

Using your journal again, list the five most influential people in your life who you know personally. For each one, ask yourself:

"Am I withholding my truth from this person in any way?" Record your feelings and observations about each of them. There's no need to act on your truth yet, unless you feel strongly that this is the time to do so. Just getting your feelings out on paper can do a lot to free up some of your blocked energy and thoughts.

Extra Nudging

If you speak your truth to your Goal Sister, and you have difficulty letting go of your expectations about how she should respond, you might consider the possibility that what's really bothering you is you. Therapists, self-help gurus, and spiritual leaders often say that what we dislike in another is often something we dislike about ourselves. It's a thought worth exploring.

Aren't you lucky? You've found someone who has your best interests at heart. She's committed to helping you maintain your goals over the long haul. She's willing to be honest and open with you. She considers your feelings and supports you through all the changes in your life. She invites a conversation that lets you know she continues to value your opinions. She models great boundaries and limits with integrity and loving kindness. Give thanks; she's your Goal Sister!

Chapter 10 Summary

★ Setbacks are common on the path to your goals, especially when you've been working toward them for a while. Be supportive of each other if you or your Goal Sister lapse.

It's okay to take a break from your focused efforts and return to working at the same intensity when you're ready.

★ You might experience a plateau in your goal achievement; you have maintained your efforts, yet you aren't seeing any visible changes or results. A goal plateau may mean that you need to adjust how you work toward your goals. It might also be a signal for you to readjust your expectations.

★ You can continue to use the Goal Sister process when big changes occur in your lives. Whether one of you moves away, starts a new job, or endures a major loss, your friendship can survive and thrive if you increase your level of encouragement, normalize each other's stress levels, and remind each other to use calming coping strategies.

★ When you react strongly to a choice your Goal Sister is making, don't be afraid to speak your truth. Be honest, kind, and candid in your communications. Disagreements often lead to greater clarity. Consider the possibility that you may be experiencing uncertainty about your own choices.

Questions

★ *How do you want your Goal Sister to support you when you experience a big change in your life?*

★ *What truth do you most need to speak to your Goal Sister right now?*

Chapter 11

Endings, Schmendings!

F ew friendships are as multifaceted as the one you have with your Goal Sister. She stands beside you through your successes and your hard times. She's honest with you. She supports you and teaches you new ways to cope with life's happenings. She recognizes your talents, points out your strengths, and helps you move through your mistakes with grace. She calls you on your limiting beliefs and reaches out a hand when you fall into your emotional holes. Yet, like any relationship, you and your Goal Sister may encounter ebbs and flows over time. Spending time together may not energize you as much as it once did. Changes in your life might pull your focus away from your goals and your Goal Sister friendship. You may come to a place where you wonder, "How long are we going to do this?" The answer will be different for each of you. To gain clarity, complete the following exercise together.

Exercise 11.1: Take Time to Reflect

If you and your Goal Sister have been meeting for a significant amount of time, schedule a time with your Goal Sister within the next week to discuss your current view of your friendship and to share your current concerns, needs, and wants. Your conversation might start with a simple question, like "Hey, how come you've been so distracted lately?" She might have a simple response, like "I know; I'm sorry about that. I'll be less distracted once this project is over." If either of you are dissatisfied with the status of your Goal Sister friendship, cite specific ways in which your current needs and wants aren't being met. Make sure you allow enough time for both of you to share your stories and give each other feedback on where you think your friendship is heading

Before you close your meeting, we suggest that you each make a heart from scrap paper using your favorite colored markers. Give each other the hearts you create, along with an affirmation or short note of appreciation. These hearts represent your commitment to the next phase of your journey together as Goal Sisters. When we speak from our heart, we gain greater understanding and compassion. Go ahead, Goal Sister, share your heart!

Maintaining Your Goal Sister Friendship

Just as you and your Goal Sister made a commitment to work toward your goals together, we encourage you to commit to facing the possible ebb and flow in your friendship. Most of you will choose to stay in the friendship and endure the bumps in the road that may come with this decision. If you haven't already touched base with each other about changes you'd like to make in your friendship, we suggest that you raise the issue every six months. Renegotiate how often you will meet and connect with each other and how you want to continue keeping each other accountable. Discuss any other expectations and needs you both have. This conversation may happen naturally after you or your Goal Sister have worked intensely toward a goal or after several years of meeting regularly. Whenever either of you feels the urge to reevaluate or shift the tenor of your interactions, don't hesitate to do so.

Goal Sister Group Story

The first Goal Sister group was designed as an eight-week pilot group to test the concepts that we've written about in this book.

At the seventh meeting of the group, Ann introduced the idea of designing a great ending for the group. How could we end our time together in a big way to honor the process and the changes we had made? Did we want to go out to dinner together? Or perhaps we would hold a potluck meal, including significant others to celebrate their support of the process? Ann left it open for discussion.

No rush of ideas poured forth. Instead there was only a sad silence. Finally, MJ said, "I really don't want the group to end!" The rest of us heaved a sigh of relief. Cindy asked, "Do we have to?" Joy wondered, "Couldn't we meet once a month?" Karen offered, "We could take turns bringing snacks." And Deborah affirmed, "I think these ideas are good, and we should keep meeting!"

What was it that sealed such a connection? When we did our group review, the Goal Sister group members identified the following feelings about the experience:

- "This group helped me learn to take control of my life."

- "I think of this group as visionaries, and I like being part of that."

- "I want to keep hearing other people's dreams so that I can learn to dream again myself."
- "My attitude has changed."
- "It opened up my world."

And so the original Goal Sisters group continues today. It has turned into an ongoing group of committed women who like what we experience together and don't want it to end!

Finding Other Goal Sisters

You might both decide to enhance your current Goal Sister friendship by including others, or you may want to find other Goal Sisters on your own. You'll intuitively know the right next step for you and your Goal Sister. Trust the process!

Michelle's Story

During a particularly difficult time of my life, when Ann and I didn't know which publisher was going to show an interest in this book, my family hadn't moved all the way into our new home, and I wasn't getting as much support as I needed for managing all my stress, I took a business trip to Washington, D.C., for my research job. I flew through Chicago and stayed with my friends Tomas and Frank for two days. I've known Tomas since graduate school, and we both worked on the same national research study. I took advantage of my trip through Chicago to meet with Tomas in person during the mornings, and he went to his office in the afternoons.

Frank's mother, Lucy, was also in town visiting from Florida. I had met her before, but we hadn't chatted much. This time, we struck up a conversation that started with "How's your family?" and quickly progressed to "Oh my gosh, you're a writer, too!" I discovered that Lucy had written and self-published a children's book, Kenyo Finds a Mission, *and that she'd written another manuscript about her life as a young mother. The more we talked, the more excited we got — and the more we wanted to fill every minute we had together talking about writing. Lucy was interested in the Goal Sister concept and our book about it. Describing the Goal Sister process to her reignited my enthusiasm for querying more publishing companies. Our time together was truly a gift. Since that visit, Lucy and I have e-mailed each other, sharing news of our writing endeavors and rejection letters and forwarding inspiring messages. Lucy came into my life when I needed another writer to inspire me.*

I continued on my trip to Washington, D.C., where I attended three long days of meetings. In the evenings, I got together with friends and colleagues. I made a point of spending a big chunk of time with my friend Phil, whom I'd met at the end of a previous research study. Phil and I had immediately clicked as friends; we have a similar passion for helping people, a shared sense of humor, and a love of anything creative. When we get together, we usually talk about how we're balancing our personal, family, and professional lives with our creative yearnings. It's great to get Phil's perspective, and I know he appreciates mine as well. Phil is an inspiration to me because he's done more than talk about creative yearnings; he's actually landed acting roles, written poetry, and gotten published! When I told Phil about my time with Lucy, he pointed out that I got what I needed: support to inspire me about this book and a new writing Goal Sister to boot. He was right. In that moment, I also realized that Phil, for all practical purposes, has been my Goal Brother. He's been there at key points in my life, encouraging me, helping me reframe my feelings of being stuck, and holding my creative dreams. I am so grateful.

I returned home from that trip with more than I left with. I was in a better place to handle my in-between feelings

*and circumstances. I had a better appreciation for the power
of asking for support and receiving it in surprising ways. And
I had two more Goal Siblings out there, supporting me and
urging me on!*

As Michelle's story illustrates, finding and connecting with
another Goal Sister — or Goal Brother — may happen "accidentally." We encourage you to be ready for these serendipitous occurrences by keeping your eyes and ears open. Just as we initially
connected through our business goals, you and your next Goal
Sister will probably share similar interests and similar goals.

Deciding to Part Ways

It is possible that you and your Goal Sister will decide to end your
connection as Goal Sisters. Depending on how you've ended other
relationships, this decision may leave parts of you feeling okay,
free, and accepting — and other parts of you feeling sad, anxious,
and abandoned. No doubt, ending your relationship as Goal Sisters will bring up memories of other endings you've experienced.
We encourage you to hold your fears and doubts at bay and to
consider the ending of your Goal Sister friendship as an opportunity to shift your beliefs about endings in general.

Ann's Story

*My spiritual beliefs have influenced how I relate to friendships. Maybe because of my past family losses, I recognize that
nothing is permanent, including our friendships. I believe
that each of us is on our own soul path. We each have lessons
to learn before we can move on. I believe that we attract to
us the people and experiences we most need to learn from.
Along the way, we share it all: joy, love, sadness, anger — giving the gift of time and of ourselves. So, unlike a lot of people,
I don't believe that friendships have to last forever. I do believe*

that we can be grateful for all the experiences we shared as friends, bless each other with love, and release each other to the next experience if and when that time comes.

I've had to end friendships a couple of times in my life. It wasn't fun, because the other person wasn't always in the same place I was. I've seen egos get in the way and cause people to view the end of our friendship as a personal affront.

Yet, in order to stay in integrity with myself, I had to do a relationship review and see which friends were mutually and genuinely supportive, as opposed to those who drained my energy and thought of me as their counselor instead of their friend.

What did I get out of these endings? Some sadness, for sure. Mostly, though, I found more peace and more clarity about what I want in my life, how I want to live it, and who I want to share it with.

Ending your connection as Goal Sisters doesn't mean you have to end your friendship. You will see in our story below about ending our Goal Sister ties with Faith that you can continue being friends. The ending can affirm the fact that you have accomplished a great deal and learned a lot about yourselves, your desires, and your abilities to make things happen for yourselves. "If that's all true," you might be wondering, "why would we want to end it?" Let's look at some of the reasons.

Going Solo

You've worked on the goals you set out to work on, and now you are ready to move forward in a different way. We experienced that kind of change with our friend, Faith.

Ann and Michelle's Story

As Michelle described in chapter 1, Faith was an original Goal Sister of ours for about four years. She worked at the same agency with us. Her Large Goal when she left the agency was to start and run her own business, which she did successfully. But after three years, Faith realized that she wanted to try her hand at the corporate world, leaving us to find our way in the entrepreneurial realm. "At first, I felt almost guilty about this decision," said Faith. "I felt that I was betraying Ann and Michelle's support. But I underestimated our friendship. Ann and Michelle believed in me, no matter what path I chose to follow." Faith stopped attending our Goal Sister meetings because our discussions and our goals were mostly focused on running our respective small businesses. Although Faith chose a different course than we all originally expected, her decision not to remain a Goal Sister didn't hurt our underlying friendship. In fact, we all stayed friends after Faith started her new job.

Michelle's Story

In her new job, Faith was working as a researcher. Being a researcher myself, I found it easy to talk with Faith about her new position and compare notes about running focus groups and creating surveys. We also shared news of our families. I didn't know anyone besides Faith who had these three areas of commonality with me: running her own consulting business, working as a researcher, and being a working mom. But we didn't set goals when we discussed those subjects. Faith and I interacted as good friends, and we remain good friends to this day.

Ann's Story

I consider Faith to be one of my dearest friends. She is always willing to listen, share her opinion in a nonjudgmental way, and kindly suggest alternative solutions. And she's a lot of fun to hang out with! The fact that we no longer have the Goal Sister commitment to accountability in various areas of our life doesn't change our commitment to our friendship.

Indeed, although the three of us are now spread all over the country, we still keep in touch about our personal and professional lives. It was Faith who hosted a celebration party for Michelle's and my Illinois friends when we completed the proposal for this book. It was Faith who sent Michelle and me inspiring and supportive e-mails throughout the process of writing the proposal. It was Faith who sent special prayers and blessings for Michelle's and my final week of work prior to our manuscript deadline. And although she chose to branch off from our Goal Sister relationship, it will be Faith who gets the first copy of this book — after Michelle and me, of course!

Deciding to go solo is actually a testament to the Goal Sister process, since empowerment is a principle we stand by.

Taking a Break

It's also possible that you just want a break from the intensity of a Goal Sister friendship. Your plate may be full at work, at home, or with volunteer activities. Rather than shortchanging your Goal Sister friendship, you may feel that it's wise to take a hiatus. That is certainly a valid wish, but before you make that decision we encourage you to consider the following questions:

- Are you trying to avoid accountability for your goals and your life by creating the need for a break instead?

- Are you allowing outside demands to steal your focus from yourself and what you truly want for your life?

- Has your Goal Sister upset you for some reason, and you want to avoid a confrontation?

By honestly evaluating your need for a break, you'll be better prepared to ask for, and receive, support from others who may be more available to provide it at this time. And a heart-to-heart conversation with your Goal Sister about your needs could lead to surprising changes in the way you continue to support each other. Stay open to the possibilities! In other friendships, many women might simply decrease their level of interaction, show less of an interest in their friend's progress, or make excuses about their lapse in the friendship. But you have invested a lot in this process and this relationship. Your Goal Sister deserves the respect of honest communication about your feelings and your decision.

Extra Nudging

If you want a break from your Goal Sister friendship because you're upset about changes in your relationship and you want to avoid a confrontation, we encourage you to review the "Speaking Your Truth" section on page 223 for guidance.

Missing in Action

Here's another possible scenario: Your Goal Sister is still calling you, she still meets you at the appointed time for your Goal Sister sessions, and she still encourages you to move toward your great life. Yet when you talk or visit, you feel that she's isn't quite present.

What happens if your Goal Sister is temporarily "missing in action" due to a new project, relationship, or other big change in her life? How do you cope with your feeling that her head and heart are not in your friendship as they once were, leaving you out in the cold? We encourage you to let those feelings out, Goal Sister! Go ahead: Stomp your feet, rant and rave in your journal, cry and lament about the good old days! Releasing your feelings will allow you to acknowledge them, and that's an important part of self-care.

Following your emotional release, arrange a time to tell your Goal Sister how you feel. It may be an easy conversation, in which your Goal Sister admits that her mind hasn't been on your friendship and your goals, or it may be a difficult conversation if your "missing in action" Goal Sister is clueless about your concerns.

Chances are she has no idea that you feel she's being less than a good friend. Whether she has entered a new phase of her life, is starting a new relationship, or is undergoing big changes, she probably hasn't considered the effect of her situation on your friendship. Your open communication and absence of judgment will go a long way in determining your future together.

How can you help her understand the impact of her choices on your friendship? Is there a way to strengthen your friendship before it erodes any more? Think back to a time when your Goal Sister displayed high energy and rapt interest in your friendship. These memories can help you frame your suggestions. For example, "Last year you had more time to just pick up and go get a cup of coffee. I miss being able to do that now that you have this new job. Is there another time of day when we might do that once in a while?" Or you might attempt to meet her halfway, saying something like, "I know the school year brings on more responsibilities in relation to your kids, but I still want to find time for us to meet. What if we sat together in the school gym while your daughter practices basketball?" Your Goal Sister will appreciate your willingness to be flexible, and she'll probably find it easier to tell you her thoughts and feelings about the process and where it fits into her life now.

Exercise 11.2: Time Marches On

When you visualize the next six months, what do you see happening in your Goal Sister friendship? Imagine that you and your Goal Sister are meeting with us at a local restaurant to talk about your relationship. Imagine Michelle asking, "What has been the most significant change for both of you?" Imagine Ann inquiring, "What part of the process has not worked for each of you, and why?" Use a page in your journal to record your answers.

Depending on the responses to these questions, you might find yourselves moving toward ending your connection as Goal Sisters. If so, do this with love and without seeing your Goal Sister friendship as a failure. Your time together as Goal Sisters was a great gift to each other, and your memories are fond.

Designing a Great Ending

No matter what the reason, if you decide to end your connection as Goal Sisters, make sure that you do it with a great finale. We strongly advocate a joyous celebration. Whether it's eating out at a favorite restaurant, dancing at a neighborhood club, or picnicking at a park, take time to plan this special event together and celebrate all the goals you've achieved and maintained in your time as Goal Sisters.

Why is it important to celebrate? Why isn't it good enough to just send a quick e-mail or card? You have both grown in a number of ways, and that deserves to be commemorated with the very one who held your goals and dreams dear. Your Goal Sister friendship involved a lot of effort, time, thought, caring, and support on both of your parts, and the end of that commitment is worthy of a celebration.

What should you do at your last meeting? We suggest that you take time to review your original and current priority goals and to talk about your successes. You might also discuss the ways in which your Goal Sister's support helped make those triumphs possible. Maybe you'll exchange gifts as one last token of your journey together, or write one last motivating message in each other's calendars for the upcoming month. No matter what you do, be creative and let your ending reflect your friendship and how you've both grown through it.

Onward and Upward!

Most women we know will choose to continue their Goal Sister friendship because there are no other friendships like it. After all, who else knows and appreciates what you have experienced to achieve and maintain your success? Who else understands the sacrifices you have made to achieve your goals? Who else cheered you on, pulled you along, and never stopped believing in you? Who else but your Goal Sister! Whether she remains in that role or you both decide to end your connection as Goal Sisters but carry on as friends, your relationship will evolve into something different as you both continue to grow and learn from each other.

Ann and Michelle's Story

On June 1, 2002, a few weeks before Michelle and her family moved from Illinois to Hawaii, we committed to continue our Goal Sister friendship. To commemorate this commitment, and to celebrate several simultaneous endings and beginnings — including the completion of our book proposal and our close-together birthdays — we threw a party. Faith hosted the soirée at her home near Bloomington.

We knew that our relationship was going to change, and that this phase was coming to a close. We also knew that we were willing to continue our Goal Sister friendship no matter how great the distance. The following e-mail exchange illustrates that commitment:

5/31/02
From: AL
To: MBP

The car is loaded and I'm ready to hit the road. Each mile will bring me closer to you, Bart, and the kids — before the miles separate us even more. I want you to know that there will never be enough miles to truly separate us. I am so grateful that we'll be celebrating our accomplishments with Faith and our other friends this weekend! And I look forward to reflecting on our years together and setting new goals at our final Goal Sister meeting in Illinois. I know we'll never stop setting and achieving goals together. I actually look forward to this new beginning. I'm focusing on the feelings of each moment. It is fine. All is well.

6/2/02
From: MBP
To: AL

Well, my friend, you pulled out of my driveway about half an hour ago, and you're on your way back to Missouri. I'm sitting here taking it all in, trying not to think too much and just be. And it's okay. I'm okay. We're going to be okay with the greater distance between us, because nothing can sever the connection we have: our friendship, our laughter, our memories, our future. What's another couple thousand miles anyway?

My tears are coming now. They're not here just because I'm sad. They're also here because I'm so grateful for all we've done and all that's ahead of us. As the card on my wall by Jean Christie Lien says, "I love this part of my life as much as the beginning. These are the 'yes' years, when there is so much we can do."

You, too, have much in your Goal Sister friendship to be grateful for. Like your close childhood girlfriends, you and your Goal Sister share an important bond; you offer each other your shoulder to lean on, your smile and words of encouragement, your interest and investment in each other's success, your gentle nudging to keep each other on track with your goals, and your sense of fun and adventure. We encourage you to continue saying "yes" to growing your friendship and reaping the rewards of this special bond. Onward and upward!

Chapter 11 Summary

★ Check in about your Goal Sister friendship every six months. If necessary, renegotiate how often you meet or talk, how you want to keep each other accountable, and any other expectations and needs you may both have.

★ If your Goal Sister is missing in action, or if you want a type of support that your Goal Sister can't give you right now, you might want another Goal Sister. Use these new friendships to enhance and complement your existing Goal Sister friendship.

★ If you decide to end your connection as Goal Sisters, celebrate joyously. You have both grown in a number of ways, and that deserves to be commemorated with the person who has held your goals and dreams dear.

★ Most women will choose to continue their Goal Sister friendship. After all, there are so few friendships like the one you have with her! No matter how you choose to move forward, as Goal Sisters or just good friends, you will both continue to grow and learn from each other.

Questions

★ *How have you handled big changes or ended friendships in the past?*

★ *How do you want to see your Goal Sister friendship evolve?*

Goal Sister Principles

We believe that you can:

- Start where your strengths are
- Release the limiting beliefs that have held you back
- Increase your awareness of your "stuff" and work through it
- Work toward your goals alone, see what happens, and then ask for support
- Hold the high vision for your Goal Sister
- Practice acceptance and give thanks for all that you are accomplishing

We believe in YOU!

Goal Sister Resources

Books

Beck, Charlotte Joko. *Everyday Zen*. San Francisco: Harper San Francisco, 1989. Interesting ways to deal with your limiting thoughts and distractions.

Bender, Sue. *Everyday Sacred: A Woman's Journey Home*. New York: HarperCollins, 1995. Beautifully written, spiritual, and thought-provoking.

Boland, Jack. *And That's the Way It Really Is! Transforming Your Desires into Reality*. Boston: MasterMind Publishing, 1997. Highly motivational, practical suggestions for creating a great life.

Cameron, Julia. *The Artist's Way: A Spiritual Path to Higher Creativity*. New York: Jeremy P. Tarcher/Putnam, 1992. A great process for jump-starting your creativity and breaking through your creative blocks.

Canfield, Jack and Mark Victor Hanson. *The Aladdin Factor*. New York: Berkley Books, 1995. Fun ways to ask for what you want.

Capacchione, Lucia. *Visioning: 10 Steps to Designing the Life of Your Dreams*. New York: J.P. Tarcher, 2000. Fun techniques for visually nudging yourself forward.

Catalfo, Phil. *Raising Spiritual Children in a Material World: Introducing Spirituality into Family Life.* New York: Berkley Books, 1997. An easy-to-read, helpful guide for parents of all denominations.

Cruise, Jorge. *Eight Minutes in the Morning: A Simple Way to Shed Up to Two Pounds a Week Guaranteed.* New York: HarperCollins, 2003. Simple yet effective exercises for a person who is busy or new to exercising.

Ellis, Dave. *Creating Your Future: Five Steps to the Life of Your Dreams.* Boston: Houghton Mifflin Company, 1998. A simple formula for goal achievement.

————. *Falling Awake: Creating the Life of Your Dreams.* Rapid City, SD: Breakthrough Enterprises, 2000. Tons of thought-provoking exercises to help you prioritize your next steps to a great life.

Ellis, Keith. *The Magic Lamp: Goal Setting for People Who Hate Setting Goals.* New York: Three Rivers Press, 1998. A quick read and a fresh approach to goal setting.

Falter-Barns, Suzanne. *How Much Joy Can You Stand? A Creative Guide to Facing Your Fears and Making Your Dreams Come True.* New York: Ballantine Wellspring, 2000. Short essays that motivate and inspire.

————. *Living Your Joy: A Practical Guide to Happiness.* New York: Ballantine, 2003. Helpful tips on how to find the time to make changes and use creative means to get there.

Gottman, John and Jan Silver. *The Seven Principles for Making Marriage Work: A Practical Guide from the Country's Foremost Relationship Expert.* New York: Crown Publishers, Inc., 1999. Well-researched information for all kinds of intimate partnerships.

Greene, Bob and Oprah Winfrey. *Make the Connection: Ten Steps to a Better Body — and a Better Life.* New York: Hyperion, 1996. Useful, informative ways to think about and structure your exercise and health routines.

Heim, Pat and Susan Murphy, with Susan K. Golant. *In the Company of Women: Indirect Aggression among Women: Why We Hurt Each Other and How to Stop.* New York: Jeremy P. Tarcher/Putnam, 2003. Well-researched and practical advice on how to deal with conflictual relationships with other women.

Kabat-Zinn, Jon. *Wherever You Go, There You Are: Mindfulness Meditation in Everyday Life.* New York: Hyperion, 1994. Great for inspiring daily mindfulness.

Klauser, Henriette Anne. *Write It Down, Make It Happen: Knowing What You Want — and Getting It!* New York: Fireside, 2000. Practical, conversational advice on how to get what you want by writing it down.

Maddox, Rebecca. *Inc. Your Dreams: For Any Woman Who Is Thinking about Her Own Business.* Audio cassette. New York: Penguin, 1995. The best way to find out if you're cut out to run your own business.

Metcalf, Franz. *What Would Buddha Do? 101 Answers to Life's Daily Dilemmas.* Berkeley, CA: Seastone, 1999. Thought-provoking and entertaining.

Phillips, Jan. *Marry Your Muse: Making a Lasting Commitment to Your Creativity.* Wheaton, IL: Quest Books, 1997. A spiritual and inspirational process.

Piercy, Day. *Day's Creating Your Life Notebook.* Chicago: CreateNet, 1996. Thoughtful, insightful approach to clarifying your goals.

Richardson, Cheryl. *Life Makeovers: 52 Practical & Inspiring Ways to Improve Your Life One Week at a Time.* New York: Broadway Books, 2000. Fun, insightful activities to change how you see and live your life.

———. *Take Time for Your Life.* New York: Broadway Books, 1998. Offers motivating exercises designed to enhance self-care.

Rubin, Harriet. *Soloing: Realizing Your Life's Ambition.* New York: Harper Business, 1999. Practical considerations for people beginning their own business.

St. John, Noah. *Permission to Succeed: Unlocking the Mystery of Success Anorexia.* Deerfield Beach, FL: Health Communications, Inc., 1999. Great information on breaking through your fears of success.

SARK. *The Bodacious Book of Succulence: Daring to Live Your Succulent Wild Life!* New York: Fireside, 1998. A colorful way to learn about yourself and journaling methods.

Sher, Barbara with Annie Gottlieb. *Wishcraft: How to Get What You Really Want.* New York: Ballantine Books, 1979. A practical goal-setting approach, with lots of examples of how different people have accomplished their goals.

Simonton, O. Carl, M.D. and Reid Henson, with Brenda Hampton.

The Healing Journey. New York: Bantam, 1992. A personal, practical story of triumph over adversity and using the power of the mind to achieve success.

Ulrich, David. *The Widening Stream: The Seven Stages of Creativity.* Hillsboro, OR: Beyond Words Publishing, 2002. A balanced, well-researched approach to understanding and igniting your creativity.

Ursiny, Tim. *The Coward's Guide to Conflict: Empowering Solutions for Those Who Would Rather Run Than Fight.* Naperville, IL: Sourcebooks, 2003. A psychologically oriented approach to reframing and approaching conflict; lots of examples.

Magazines

Fast Company (www.fastcompany.com). Articles on business trends.

Inc. (www.inc.com). Very helpful articles, written by or about people who have succeeded or failed at starting and running their own businesses.

Mary Engelbreit's Home Companion (www.maryengelbreit.com/MEHC/). Lots of whimsy and fun ideas, and an inspiring Artist's Workshop feature.

O: The Oprah Magazine (www.oprah.com). Consistently presents celebrity and everyday people's stories on how to live your best life.

Shape (www.shapeonline.com). Uplifting personal stories and a great balance of articles and recommended exercises for the mind, body, and soul.

Spirituality and Health (www.spiritualityhealth.com). Offers helpful articles and features on having a balanced life.

Working Mother (www.workingmother.com). A quick way to get information about how to successfully juggle being a working mom.

Acknowledgments

Writing this book has been an emotionally satisfying and trying experience for both of us. We could not have accomplished this feat without our trusty personal computers, DSL connections, and the support of many people. Together, we sincerely thank:

- Faith Russell, for your confidence in our abilities to write this book and for cheering us on all the way. We appreciate you so much!

- The original Goal Sister Group members, Deborah Adkins, Joy Hensley, Michelle Jones (MJ), Karen McGlamery, Cindy Mauller, Nelda Patrick, and Arlene Sadowski, for participating in the pilot process, for showing us new ways to be successful, and for being our awesome Goal Sisters.

- Renée Beaulieu, Robin Haskins, Kate Hein, Phil Meyer, Susie Olson, MaryLu Stefan, and Laurie Stewart, for reading and providing comments on the early drafts of our book proposal. Your enthusiasm spurred us on!

- Laurie Stewart and Roger Stewart, for sharing your publishing wisdom and experience with us throughout the submission and publication process.

- The crew at New World Library, specifically: Georgia Hughes, for believing in us and in Goal Sisters and for allowing us to collaborate with you in the production of this book; Kristen Cashman and Carol Venolia, for your careful editing and thoughtful comments — your input helped make this book shine; Mary Ann Casler, for capturing the feel of the Goal Sister process with your design of the cover; and Munro Magruder and Monique Muhlenkamp, for your energy and enthusiasm around spreading the word about Goal Sisters.

Ann is grateful to the following:

- God, my business and life partner. It is the Father within who does the work.

- Michelle Beaulieu Pillen, for sharing a vision of something bigger for our lives, supporting me in dreaming BIG, and encouraging me to leap at the right time.

- Ted Gillespie, for his love and support. I am grateful for our shared experiences in accepting, laughing, trusting, and loving. You remind me to find my center.

- Arlese Bradley, for her prayers, her belief in only the highest good for all of us, and her unwavering trust in the divine plan for this book and our lives.

- The Mastermind partners who have held my prayers sacred: Suzi Back, Andrea Coleman, Toni Corrigan, Kimbra Crowder, Pat Fenix, Jarie Ford, Ted Gillespie, Janet Johnson, Michelle Jones, Marsha McChan, Theresa Maria Napa, Amber Obloj, Brooke Ray, Linda Kimber Weber, and Magge Young.

- Earl Mace and Nancy Kremer, my personal life coaches who inspired me to stretch even more in creating my great life. Earl: like Truman, I am walking through the door! Nancy: I am declaring my intentions even more clearly, thanks to you!

- The many friends who jumped in to say "yes, you can!" including: Sherry Boyer, Ruth Cobb, Wayne Dunard, Kate and Ed Hein, Shane Knox, Paula Pillen, Karen Pope, Lee Radcliff, Margaret Scrogham, and Pat Worley.

- Members of the LifeSupport Ministries support groups who teach me daily that the little steps can sometimes make the biggest difference.

- Steve Willis and the memory of Tony Miller, two men who reminded me that there is no distance between those who are truly friends.

- Robert "Beau" Johnson, who encouraged me early in life to hear the call of the open road and who to this day urges me to follow it.

- My deceased parents, Dorothy and Bill Leach, who entrusted me with the gifts of creativity, humor, integrity, love, and compassion before the end of their much-too-short time here on earth.

Michelle gives special thanks to the following:

- Ann Leach, for encouraging me many years ago when I was unsure of myself, for nudging me to create art, and for being my Goal Sister and writing partner.

- Bart, Zoë, and Kanoa Pillen, for understanding that this book had to be written now. Thanks Zoë and Kanoa, for being great kids and for reminding me to make time to play. Thanks Bart, for your enduring love, faith, and support.

- Bill and Jan Beaulieu, for all you have given me and for being there for Zoë and Kanoa when I wasn't available to attend soccer games and help with homework.

- Shane Knox, Phil Meyer, Natalie Pillen, and Tomas Soto, for being my "go to" comrades through thick and thin. You all help me daily to stay the course.

- Lucy Lefevre, for being my writing Goal Sister and for sending me heartfelt prayers and encouragement.

- Sue Bender, Julia Cameron, Anne Lamott, Rebecca Maddox, and Alice Walker, for sharing your insights and experiences with the world, and for inspiring me.

Index

260 index

About the Authors

Ann Leach, M.A., is a life coach, group facilitator, and writer. She has worked as a theater publicist and has counseled people living with cancer, AIDS, and substance abuse. Ann currently provides workshops on burnout and facilitates support groups for people living with depression. She writes for several regional magazines, and she self-published a children's book. Ann lives in southwestern Missouri.

Michelle Beaulieu Pillen, Ph.D., has worked as a therapist, program evaluator, and researcher for the past eighteen years in the mental health, HIV, and substance abuse fields. With the publication of *Goal Sisters,* Michelle is adding writer and artist to her résumé. She lives in Hawaii with her husband, their two children, their two cats, and their dog.

How to Contact the Goal Sisters

We would love to hear from you! Whether you want to tell us how you're doing with the Goal Sister process or are interested in having us facilitate a woman's retreat or speak at your event, please visit our website at **www.goalsisters.com**. We also welcome your e-mails and phone calls.

You can e-mail Ann at ann@goalsisters.com or call her at (417) 624-3363.

You can e-mail Michelle at michelle@goalsisters.com or call her at (808) 262-2796.

Onward and upward!

New World Library is dedicated to
publishing books and audio products
that inspire and challenge us to improve
the quality of our lives and our world.

Our products are available
in bookstores everywhere.
For our catalog, please contact:

New World Library
14 Pamaron Way
Novato, California 94949

Phone: (415) 884-2100 or (800) 972-6657
Catalog requests: Ext. 50
Orders: Ext. 52
Fax: (415) 884-2199

E-mail: escort@newworldlibrary.com
Website: www.newworldlibrary.com